the
home owner's
manual

[installation]   [maintenance]

[investment]   [improvement]

the home
owner's manual

OPERATING INSTRUCTIONS, TROUBLESHOOTING
TIPS, AND ADVICE ON HOUSEHOLD MAINTENANCE

by Dan Ramsey and the Fix-It Club®

Illustrated by Paul Kepple and Jude Buffum

QUIRK BOOKS
PHILADELPHIA

Text copyright © 2006 by Dan Ramsey

Illustrations copyright © 2006 by Headcase Design

Library of Congress Cataloging in Publication Number: Requested

ISBN: 1-59474-103-4

Printed in Singapore

Typeset in Swiss

Designed by Paul Kepple and Jude Buffum @ Headcase Design
www.headcasedesign.com

Distributed in North America by Chronicle Books
85 Second Street
San Francisco, CA 94105

10 9 8 7 6 5 4 3 2 1

Quirk Books
215 Church Street
Philadelphia, PA 19106
www.quirkbooks.com

Contents

WELCOME TO YOUR NEW HOME! 12
The Home: Diagram and Parts List 15
Product Life Span 21

CHAPTER 1:
DESCRIPTION 23

Product History 24
Major Components 25
  ▪ Functional Spaces 25
  ▪ Interconnections 26
  ▪ Dimensions 26
  ▪ Design Philosophy 27
Ownership Advantages 28
  ▪ Easier Living 28
  ▪ Investment Opportunities 28
  ▪ Tax Advantages 28
Ownership Disadvantages 29
Ownership Options 29
  ▪ Single-Family Residence 29
  ▪ Planned-Unit Development 30
  ▪ Condominium Apartment 30
  ▪ Cooperative Apartment 30
Top-Selling Models 31
Home Design Trends 36
  ▪ Environmentally Friendly Design 36
  ▪ Off-Site Construction 36
  ▪ Adaptive Reuse 37
  ▪ Health-Conscious Designs 37
  ▪ Weather Resistance 38
  ▪ Flexible Floor Plans 38
  ▪ Accessibility 38

- Outdoor Living 39
- Abundant Storage 39
- Cultural Upgrades 39

CHAPTER 2:
INSTALLATION 41

Installing Occupants 42
Determining Occupant Requirements 42
- Selecting by Type 43
- Determining Usage 48
- Choosing a Location 50
- Analyzing Condition 52
Home Pre-Acquisition Inspection Checklist 54
Shopping for a Home 58
- Using Agents 58
- Buying FSBOs 60
- Closing on a Home 61
Paying for a Home 62
- Cash Talks 62
- Conventional Financing 63
- Unconventional Financing 64
Moving In 64
- Moving Companies 65
- Self Moves 65
- Component Services 67
- Moving On 67

CHAPTER 3:
PARTS AND SERVICE 69

Shelter Requirements 70
- Structural 70
- Electrical 74

- Plumbing 78
- Heating 80
- Cooling 82
- Security 83
Benefits of Maintenance 83
Maintenance Materials 84
- Structural 84
- Electrical 85
- Plumbing 85
- Heating and Cooling 86
Selecting and Using Tools and Fasteners 86
Shopping in a Hardware Store 88

CHAPTER 4:
INTERIOR MAINTENANCE 91

Maintaining Home Interiors 92
Structural Maintenance 93
- Cleaning 93
- Maintaining Carpets 94
- Maintaining Door Locks 95
- Painting the Interior 96
- Filling Surface Holes 99
Electrical Maintenance 100
- Inspecting Receptacles and Switches 100
- Inspecting Cords for Damage 101
- Checking All Circuit Breakers or Fuses 103
- Testing GFCI outlets 104
Plumbing Maintenance 105
- Treating Slow Drains 105
- Checking Pipes and Fixtures for Leaks 106
- Draining Sludge from Water Heater 107
- Testing Water Heater Relief Valve 108

Heating and Cooling Maintenance 110
  ■ Inspecting Systems 110
  ■ Cleaning Ductwork 111
  ■ Cleaning or Replacing Filters 112
  ■ Checking Fans, Belts, and Motors 113
  ■ Cleaning a Chimney 114
  ■ Cleaning Humidifiers and Dehumidifiers 116
  ■ Cleaning Radiators 117
  ■ Bleeding Air from Hot Water Heating Systems 118
Safety Maintenance 118
  ■ Checking Fire Extinguishers 118
  ■ Testing Smoke Detectors 120
  ■ Practicing Emergency Drills 120
  ■ Replenishing the Survival Pantry 121

CHAPTER 5:
EXTERIOR MAINTENANCE 123

Maintaining Home Exteriors 124
Roofing 125
  ■ Checking the Roof for Damage 125
  ■ Checking the Attic for Water Stains 126
  ■ Cleaning Gutters 127
Siding 128
  ■ Cleaning Siding 128
  ■ Inspecting for Pests and Damage 130
  ■ Painting Siding 131
Doors and Windows 132
  ■ Replacing Damaged or Worn Weather Stripping 132
  ■ Recaulking Windows, Doors, and Siding 133
  ■ Checking Window Seals 133
Decks 134
  ■ Pressure Washing Decks 134

- Recoating Decks 135
Patios, Walks, and Drives 139
- Pressure Washing Patios, Walks, and Drives 139
- Patching Surfaces 140
Yard Maintenance 140
Outdoor Storage Structures 142
- Maintaining Siding 142
- Maintaining Doors and Hinges 142
Garages 143
- Cleaning Garage Floors 143
- Patching Concrete 144
- Maintaining Garage Doors 145

CHAPTER 6:
EMERGENCY REPAIRS 147

Avoiding Emergencies 148
Structural Emergencies 148
- Damaged Siding 148
- Rotten or Eaten Wood 149
- Leaky Roof 150
Electrical Emergencies 151
- Fixing Appliances 151
- Restoring Electrical Power 152
Plumbing Emergencies 154
- Leaky Faucet 154
- Clogged Kitchen Drain 156
- Clogged Bathroom Drain 158
- Clogged Toilet 159
- Broken Pipes 160
- Leaky Basement 161
- No Hot Water 162
- Leaky Water Heater 163

Heating and Cooling Emergencies 164
- Fuel Leak 164
- No Heat 164
- No Cooling 165

CHAPTER 7:
OPTIONS 169

Decorating Basics 170
Interior Painting 170
- Preparing Surfaces 170
- Choosing Paints 172
- Selecting and Using Painting Tools 174
- Selecting Other Painting Materials 175
- The Painting Process 176
- Cleaning Up 177
Wall Coverings 179
- Preparing Surfaces 179
- Installing Wallpaper 180
Flooring 182
- Installing Carpeting 182
- Installing Hardwood Flooring 183
- Installing Hard Tile 185
- Installing VCT 188
Getting Professional Help 189

CHAPTER 8:
UPGRADES 191

Remodeling Benefits 192
Remodeling Basics 194
Remodeling a Kitchen 197
Remodeling a Bathroom 205
Remodeling an Extra Room 208

APPENDIX 213
Technical Support 214
Glossary of Terms 215

INDEX 218

OWNER'S CERTIFICATE 223

ABOUT THE AUTHOR 224
ABOUT THE ILLUSTRATORS 224

Welcome
to Your New Home!

ATTENTION!

Before beginning this manual, please inspect your model carefully and check for all of the standard parts described on pages 15–21. If any of these parts appears to be missing or inoperative, it is recommended that you consult the home's builder or appropriate service providers immediately.

Whether you have just acquired a new home or are planning to do so soon, congratulations! A home is a wonderful thing to inhabit, particularly when it is owned—and it is in good working order.

Unfortunately, components break, wear out, and mysteriously go awry, especially when homeowners share their residence with occupants who don't pay the repair bills. And if homeowners spend most of their time in the world of high technology, the processes and problems of low-tech homes may elude them. Regrettably, homes don't come with instruction manuals, so homeowners are left on their own to unclog a sink, maintain cozy heat, or make the lights come back on. To make matters worse, many first-time buyers don't know what to look for in a home before purchasing one. Nor are there instructions for upgrading to Home 2.0.

Until now, that is. This manual includes not only an overview of how a home works, but also many step-by-step instructions on what to do if it doesn't—or if the occupants decide to make some changes. It also includes some practical tips on selecting and moving into a first or next home. Like other owner's manuals, it is designed for quick and frequent reference. Unlike other manuals, this book is printed on heavy paper to stand up to frequent use. Here's what is covered:

DESCRIPTION (pages 23–39) describes the major functions of homes as well as the advantages and options of ownership.

INSTALLATION (pages 41–67) explains the home selection and occupant-installation processes.

PARTS AND SERVICE (pages 69–89) explains how home systems operate and interact to furnish comfort and convenience to occupants.

INTERIOR MAINTENANCE (pages 91–121) offers specific instructions for 25 common maintenance projects inside the home, including keeping plumbing clear, maintaining electrical and heating systems, painting, and more.

EXTERIOR MAINTENANCE (pages 123–145) includes step-by-step instructions for 19 common projects for the home's exterior, including roofing, siding, doors and windows, decks, patios and walks, yard maintenance, and storage structures.

EMERGENCY REPAIRS (pages 147–167) is a quick and easy reference for handling 16 common home emergencies in plumbing, electrical, heating, and structural systems.

OPTIONS (pages 169–189) suggests popular improvements that will make a home more livable and gives specific instructions on how to complete them.

UPGRADES (pages 191–211) covers numerous things that homeowners can do—or have done for them—to increase the functionality and value of a home.

The **APPENDIX** (pages 213–215) includes technical support resources and a glossary of housing terminology.

When maintained properly, a home can furnish years of living comfort and convenience for current and future occupants. Remember that homes require an investment of time, energy, and money that may make occupants reconsider renting. However, a home is a long-term investment that offers financial and emotional rewards beyond those available through rent receipts.

Congratulations and welcome to the world of home ownership!

The Home:
Diagram and Parts List

Major home systems: structural, electrical, plumbing, comfort. Each of these systems has an important function. To ensure that these functions are met, modern homes must be built to standardized rules, called *building codes*, for safety. Older homes typically are required to "come up to code" if remodeled. Codes are especially important for standardizing the safe use of electrical, plumbing, and other vital systems.

Structural

The primary system within a home is the structural skeleton. It includes:

Foundation: A concrete structure that firmly attaches the house to the ground and distributes the structure's weight.

Framing: The wood, steel, or masonry skeleton that forms the floors, walls, and ceilings of the home.

Exterior: The sheathing or skin over the outside of the framing as well as the exterior barriers (doors and windows).

Interior: The sheathing or covering over the inside of the framing as well as the interior barriers (doors).

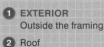

1. **EXTERIOR**
   Outside the framing
2. Roof
3. Windows
4. Sheathing
5. Doors

6. **INTERIOR**
   Inside the framing
7. Stairs
8. Ceiling
9. Walls: loadbearing or non
10. Flooring: carpet, wood, or tile
11. Doors

12. **FRAMING**
    Can be wood, steel, or masonry
13. Joists and subfloor
14. Top and bottom plate
15. Studs

16. **FOUNDATION**
    Attaches home to the ground
17. Rebar reinforces structure
18. Space for service systems

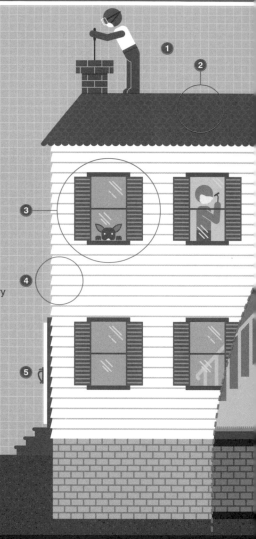

HOME STRUCTURAL COMPONENTS: All homes should consist

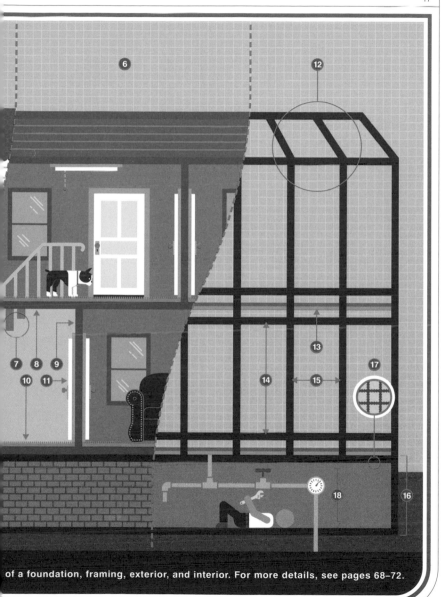

of a foundation, framing, exterior, and interior. For more details, see pages 68–72.

Electrical

Modern homes rely on electricity to power appliances and lighting. Electrical power is generated in power plants and distributed through wires as alternating current (ac). The electricity is moved along the wires by voltage, electrical pressure measured in volts (v). The voltage is reduced by transformers until it reaches residences at 240 v. Electric clothes dryers and some shop equipment use 240 v of electricity, but everything else in the home uses 120 v, so the electrical power is cut in half at the electric service panel.

⚠ *CAUTION: Residents who attempt to work on a home's electrical system should know how it functions, how to disable it, and how to perform maintenance safely—all covered in this manual.*

From the electric service panel, numerous branches of power, called *circuits*, are distributed through wires. These wires start within the service panel at a circuit breaker and end within the house at outlets (plugs) or fixtures (lights). The circuit breakers are safety devices designed to stop the flow of electricity if it exceeds what the wire and fixtures can safely handle. (Homes older than 40 years may use replaceable fuses instead of circuit breakers.) Fixtures typically have a switch nearby that allows the circuit to be turned on or off manually. Large and small appliances can be attached (plugged in) to outlets to draw electrical power required for operation.

Electrical systems can be seen at either end (the service panel and the fixture), but are unseen; the wires are run through walls, floors, and ceilings. Because electrical systems have no moving parts, maintenance and repair typically is done at one end or the other of the circuits, making them relatively easy to maintain (see page 100–105).

Plumbing

Plumbing is a distribution system that delivers fresh water to plumbing fixtures and separately removes the waste water for treatment. Water is distributed by utility services through water pipelines under the ground in front of homes. Alternatively, private water systems can gather and deliver water from springs or wells. Water moves through a pipe and water meter to individual homes and is distributed throughout the house by smaller pipes to kitchen, bath, utility, and other rooms as needed. Fixtures (faucets, toilets) manually start and stop the flow of water at these locations.

A portion of the incoming water supply is routed to the water heater for heat and storage. A second set of distribution pipes delivers the hot water to selected fixtures (kitchen and bathroom sinks) and appliances (dishwasher) within the home. The remainder of the fresh or supply water serves the cold water needs of the home.

Waste water from plumbing fixtures (sinks, toilets) flows from the drain-waste-vent (DWV) system to the public sewer or private septic tank system. The drain system allows waste water to pass without allowing waste gases to enter the room. The vent system allows waste gases to vent to the atmosphere above the home's roof.

Because plumbing systems are built following safety codes, health concerns rarely are an issue. Instead, the failure of plumbing systems typically is due to excessive use (fixture wear or blockage) or damage (a broken pipe). With knowledge and basic tools, homeowners can successfully maintain and repair most plumbing system components.

Comfort

A significant advantage of enclosed residences is the opportunity to control climate. This is the function of the home's comfort system, also known as the heating and cooling system. Depending on the model and its location, one or the other of these two interconnected systems may be more important. For example, homes located in cold climates may have extensive heating systems with little or no cooling systems. Conversely, homes in warm climates may require large cooling systems and minimal heating systems. Many homes require combination systems that can integrate both functions with single distribution systems.

Heating systems are economically dependent upon the long-term availability and cost of specific fuels. For example, in regions where hydroelectric power is available relatively inexpensively, homeowners may depend primarily on electric heat sources, especially where climate swings are not dramatic. In other locations, fossil fuel systems are the most cost-effective source of residential heat. Increasingly, homeowners are relying on renewable energy sources (solar, wind, water) to develop heat or energy for home comfort.

Heating appliances have dramatically evolved over the past 20 years as fuel costs and fuel concerns have risen. Modern heating furnaces are approaching 100 percent efficiency, meaning that all potential heat energy in the fuel is utilized. However, efficient heating systems require periodic maintenance, much of it easily done by the knowledgeable homeowner (see pages 110–118).

Cooling systems include various types of air cooling devices. Evaporation, or swamp, coolers cool air by forcing it through a layer of water vapor. Air conditioners and heat pumps cool air by removing the heat from the air, much as a refrigerator does. Fortunately, seasonal maintenance is relatively easy to perform on cooling systems.

Together, the above systems contribute to the livability of a home.

Product Life Span

Homes are generally quite long-lived, though condition varies depending on initial construction and owner maintenance. In some parts of the world, livable homes with ages of 500 years or more have been documented, though retrofitting has been ongoing. Ancient, uninhabitable homes (constructed prior to building codes) that are even older have been discovered. Typically, modern homes may live 50 to 100 and more years with proper maintenance and minor retrofitting for newer technologies. A home's natural enemies are fire, flood, earthquakes, excessive wind, and wood-damaging pests. Residential longevity depends on owner maintenance.

Chapter 1

Description

Product History

Homes, currently available in a wide variety of models (see page 31), have been utilized by humans since the dawn of time. The earliest homes were simple shelters from the weather and wild beasts. Because the food supply was movable, early human homes were portable. As humans developed agrarian lifestyles, housing became more permanent and, eventually, attached to the land. Humans began building homes in clusters for convenience and protection. With the necessary investment of effort, ownership of the land and house became more important, resulting in the birth and growth of the real estate (immovable property) industry.

Today, there are approximately 125 million housing units in the United States and 12 million in Canada. At any given time, about 10 percent are vacant, waiting for new owners, renters, or returning vacationers. The balance is split between owner occupants (two-thirds) and renter occupants (one-third). These numbers vary depending on location and occupant age. Younger city-dwellers are less likely, while older ruralites are more likely, to own their residence. However, trends have moved toward increased home ownership in nearly all locations and age groups for a variety of important reasons.

Homes are increasingly popular products that fulfill multiple physical, emotional, and psychological needs for their inhabitants. In addition, homes establish a location for other life functions previously found only outside the home: entertainment and work. Simultaneously, services traditionally provided inside the home, such as food preparation and consumption, are moving outside and even along commute paths. Yet the major components and primary functions of homes have not significantly changed in a century.

Major Components

Functional Spaces

Each component within a home is designed to fulfill at least one primary function. These components, also known as functional spaces or rooms, typically have primary, secondary, and even tertiary purposes. For example, the main living room may serve as a meeting area for residents as well as an entertainment area and even a dining area. The bathroom, depending on equipment, can serve hygiene as well as relaxation functions. The main functions of a home include:

Sustenance: Kitchen, dining area

Hygiene: Bathrooms

Rest and privacy: Bedrooms

Diversion: Living room, family room, media room, porch, patio, deck

Storage: Closets, garage, outbuildings

As home-occupant candidates begin the search for housing, they consciously or unconsciously decide the function and functionality of a specific home's spaces to meet their requirements. Is it big enough? Is it sufficiently equipped? Refer to Chapter 2 on Installation for additional factors in the livability decision.

Interconnections

In addition to functional spaces, homes require a hierarchy of room relationships with a design that efficiently interconnects these rooms. Models that have bedrooms without access, for example, are unlivable and undesirable. Also, models that are not planned for efficient traffic flow are less livable and less desirable. In contrast, a home with efficient room placement and interconnections enhances the lives of occupants.

Dimensions

The average U.S. home is approximately 2,300 square feet (214 square m), a 10 percent increase in size over the past decade. This median size takes into account smaller residences, such as townhouses (see page 30) as well as estate homes.

⚠️ **EXPERT TIP:** *A square foot (sq ft) is an area one foot (12 inches; in) by one foot (ft), or 144 square inches (sq in). A square meter (sq m) is an area one meter (m) by one meter (10,000 square centimeters; sq cm). Homes typically are measured using exterior dimensions. Room size usually is measured in interior space.*

Home sizes are on the increase due to expanded requirements. Occupants want more things within their living space. Home entertainment centers are larger, often taking up a dedicated room; kitchens include enlarged and more functional appliances; bathrooms may include hot tubs, double sinks, garden areas, and bidets.

Components within a modern home are designed for the dimension of the "typical" homeowner, with a height of 70 in (177.8 cm) and an arm span of 72 in (182.9 cm). Fortunately, most adult residents will be within 15 percent of these dimensions, thus allowing for standardized kitchen cabinetry and bathroom fixtures. However, some homes may require designing or adjustment for people with special requirements, especially in bathrooms, kitchens, doorways, and access to other levels of the home. Commercial buildings usually require designs for people with disabilities, but residences do not.

Design Philosophy

Homes are inanimate, but home designers are not. Their design philosophy will carry over into the components, interconnections, and especially the style of the residence. This is the design philosophy. In addition, each occupant group will quickly establish its own philosophy of living in the residence. The philosophy could be categorized as formal, informal, neat, chic, cluttered, or balanced.

Feng shui (pronounced *fung shway*) is an ancient Chinese philosophy focused on creating harmony and balance in life and in living areas. Though the concept is simple, the application can become complex, as advocates have established specific rules for applying feng shui in order to produce positive energy, or *ch'i*, in a home or room design. In addition, there are numerous ways to practice feng shui within a residence. Fortunately, much of it is based on common sense, with a clean and uncluttered design aimed at enhancing occupants' harmony with living components.

Ownership Advantages

Home ownership offers numerous advantages as well as a few disadvantages over renting a residence. Following are the primary advantages and disadvantages:

Easier Living

Residential structures are designed to offer convenient opportunities to fulfill basic human needs. Owning a residence allows occupants to personalize the structure and its components more than if it were a rented space. Site selection due to physical convenience to school, work, and other activities makes living easier for all inhabitants.

Investment Opportunities

Economists report that, in the United States, home values have increased 36 percent on average between 2000 and 2005, nearly three times the rate of inflation for the same period. In some areas, the increase is more than 120 percent. This year's $250,000 home typically will be worth $270,000 or more next year. It is often an excellent investment because homeowners leverage a small down payment into a high rate of return.

Tax Advantages

The portion of a mortgage that is paid toward interest on the debt, typically the majority of the payment, may be deducted from federal income tax. Discuss this option with a tax advisor.

Ownership Disadvantages

A major disadvantage to home ownership is a residence's inherent un-portability. It is expensive to move an existing home any distance due to its size, weight, complexity, and path limitations to the new location. Most homeowners instead sell the home in one location and buy in another (see page 50). More likely, persons who need to move frequently will rent residences. However, by doing so they are giving their rental fees to the residence's owners to utilize the investment and tax benefits.

Another disadvantage of home ownership is a variation on the same issue: unportability. If a home is purchased in a neighborhood of falling values, the homeowner may take a financial loss when selling the home. If easy, it would be more economical to move the house to a better neighborhood. The solution to this problem is for the home-occupant candidate to fully research all financial aspects of any considered transaction (see page 62).

Ownership Options

Single-Family Residence

Most homeowners live in single-family residences (SFRs). An SFR is a residential structure designed for use by one living group. The structure typically is detached from other homes and is commonly called a *house*. Owners have rights to use not only the house, but also the property surrounding the house identified as the lot.

Planned-Unit Development

A planned-unit development (PUD) is similar to a single-family residence except that the homes are physically attached to each other. In addition, property surrounding the unit is jointly rather than separately owned. The advantage is cost, because in some locations land lot prices are too high for homeowners to purchase individually. The disadvantage is that the neighbors are separated by a single wall rather than space. Many PUDs utilize the townhouse design with two or more levels to minimize the ground space the unit requires. Each unit in a PUD has its own entryway.

Condominium Apartment

A condominium apartment or condo is slightly different in that there are common areas within the building that are jointly owned, such as entryways and hallways. The property around the apartment building including walkways also is jointly owned and shared.

Cooperative Apartment

A cooperative apartment, or co-op, is different yet. All residents share ownership of the entire structure and land with rights to use one unit and all of the common areas. Co-ops typically are owned by corporations in which residents are shareholders.

Top-Selling Models

Homes available today include a mixture of types and styles with numerous modifications and upgrades. Therefore, there is a great diversity in the home styles available in the marketplace. Following is a list of the top-selling home designs and the era in which they were most popular.

Earth (prehistoric–present): Residences constructed of natural materials (earth, straw, cob) with a focus on minimal cost and energy efficiency.

Cape Cod (1650–1950): Originated in New England with modest designs based on scarcity of materials. Most popular are one-and-a-half story homes built during the 1930s and 1940s.

Log (1700–present): Initially spartan structures of local tree logs; currently larger homes of massive materials utilizing modern building methods.

Georgian Colonial (1700–1830): Symmetrical, orderly style popular in Colonial America. The front door is flanked by columns or pilasters (shown, page 34).

Federal (1780–1840): Graceful colonial homes with decorative columns, cornice, and facade.

Greek Revival (1825–1860): North American interpretation of Greek-like designs with elongated windows (shown, page 35).

Southern Colonial (1830–1862): Grand plantation homes of the American South prior to the Civil War (shown, page 35).

Victorian Gothic (1840–1880): Include arches, pointed windows, and other details from medieval Gothic cathedrals (shown, page 34).

Folk Victorian (1870–1910): Basic homes that utilize mass-produced trimwork emulating Victorian homes, though simpler in design.

Shingle (1874–1910): Rustic coastal housing style with gable roofs and dormer windows.

Victorian Queen Anne (1880–1910): Utilizes wrap-around porches, turrets, and other ornate details.

Colonial Revival (1880–1955): Symmetrical houses combining elements of Georgian and Federal styles, focusing on the entrance.

Beaux-Arts (pronounced *bo-zar*: 1885–1925): Lavish designs based on French architecture using grand stairways, balconies, mansard roofs, and stone exteriors.

Mission (1890–1920): Stucco walls, arches, tile roof, and other details inspired by Spanish mission churches of the American Southwest (shown, page 34).

Tudor (1890–1940): Decorative half-timbering and other details suggesting medieval architecture. Similar to Medieval Revival and English Country designs (shown, page 35).

Foursquare (1895–1930): Large, square, practical, economical style especially popular in the American and Canadian Midwest. Also referred to as *farmhouse* (shown, page 35).

Pueblo Revival (1900–present): Based on native American dwellings of the Southwest updated with modern conveniences.

Craftsman (1905–1930): Simple design developed and marketed by Sears, Roebuck, & Co. as owner-built kits (shown, page 34). Similar to Bungalow style, which utilizes large overhangs and dormer windows.

French (1915–1945): Inspired by French architecture incorporating designs from estates as well as cottages.

Prairie (1910–1950): Horizontal design elements with low roofs, deep over-hangs, and casement windows, made popular by Frank Lloyd Wright.

Ranch (1935–present): One-story design for larger property lots of the American West (shown, page 34). Variations include Western Ranch and California Rambler.

Split-Entry (1935–present): Multi-level ranch-style home (shown, page 35). One of the most popular styles in many regions of the United States; also known as Raised Ranch.

A-Frame (1957–present): Dramatic sloping roof with living quarters below and sleeping quarters above. Popular in high-snow regions.

Dome (1960–present): Monolithic and geodesic dome technology applied to home design.

Neoeclectic (1965–present): Hybrid designs offered in home plan catalogs.

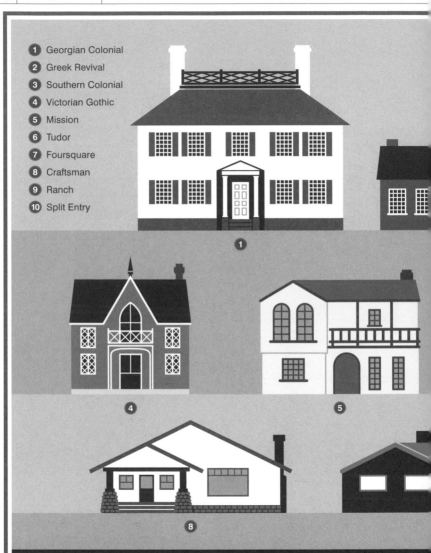

1. Georgian Colonial
2. Greek Revival
3. Southern Colonial
4. Victorian Gothic
5. Mission
6. Tudor
7. Foursquare
8. Craftsman
9. Ranch
10. Split Entry

TOP-SELLING MODELS: There are many home styles to choose from.

The models shown above represent some of the most popular designs.

There are numerous other architectural designs applied to homes. More often, modern home designs apply components from more than one style.

Home Design Trends

Home designs are intended to reflect both the needs and the tastes of occupants. They also reflect the latest building materials, codes, and techniques. Because these elements are in constant flux, the state of home design also is changing. Following are important trends in home design.

Environmentally Friendly Design

Because producers and consumers are becoming increasingly aware of the limited availability of resources, focus is intensifying on how homes and home-construction materials can be designed for less environmental impact. In addition to basic designs (earth, log, dome) that are being enhanced by technology, all other architectural designs can be made more energy-efficient and built with recycled materials. Also, renewable fuel sources (solar, wind, water) are being incorporated into new homes as well as retrofitted to older ones.

Off-Site Construction

Early homes were built using locally available materials. Eventually, materials, such as wood, were harvested, milled, and delivered regionally. Many home construction materials today travel more than 1,000 miles before becoming part of a home. The latest trend is to build components or even an entire house off-site. Manufactured homes, for example, are built in two or three sections, towed to a building site, and place on a site-built foundation. With the addition of a garage, driveway, walks, and landscaping, it becomes difficult to distinguish between a site-built and off-site-built home.

The primary advantage to off-site-built homes is cost. It is less expensive to build homes where a factory offers consistency and labor costs are lower. In fact, the only site preparation required for a manufactured home is the installation of a foundation and the final joining of the housing units. The structural, electrical, plumbing, and comfort systems are already in place and ready for connection.

Adaptive Reuse

As available space for building is taken up by new housing, many builders and buyers are turning to existing structures for adaptive reuse. Land with dilapidated structures is becoming the site of new homes. Older structures are retrofitted as new residences. Commercial buildings are repurposed into multi-family residences (MFRs).

Health-Conscious Designs

Unfortunately, some buildings can literally make occupants sick. Home designers are increasingly aware of how human health is affected by synthetic materials. Most critical are paints and composition wood products that rely on chemical additives that may be poisonous or cause allergic reactions. The latest trend in health-conscious home design is avoiding plastics, laminates, and fume-producing glues.

Weather Resistance

In some regions, the primary enemy of housing is the elements. Homes in Florida, for example, must stand up to hurricane-force winds and waves. Homes in the South and Midwest face tornados and high humidity. Northern homes must withstand the added weight of snow and the hazards of ice. Homes in the West are subject to earthquakes and land-shifting. The latest trend is to utilize the newest technologies to build homes that can withstand these elements with smarter designs and cost-effective materials.

Flexible Floor Plans

The only constant is change. The needs of home occupants typically change more frequently than a home can be adapted. What was a third bedroom becomes a game room. A garage morphs into a home office. A recent trend in home design actually is an old idea: multi-purpose rooms. Many early homes were designed as a few rooms that could easily be modified to fit growing families and their needs. For example, kitchens and bedrooms were constructed with no built-ins. Pantries and closets were freestanding and could be moved to other rooms in the house as needs changed. Today's home designs often incorporate this concept to allow today's home office to become tomorrow's media center.

Accessibility

Universal design is the latest attempt to make homes accessible to more people. In addition to building homes with dimensions, floors, cabinets, and fixtures that can be used by those with disabilities, designers also understand that people come in all sizes and shapes.

Doorways are wider, window sills are lower, and cabinets are easier to access by all.

Outdoor Living

In most climates, outdoor living is on the increase. Eco-friendly architecture is integrating outdoor spaces into the overall home design. Decks, yards, and gardens are becoming components within a home's floor plan. Secondary kitchens and even bedrooms are incorporated into decks and patios to extend a home's livability.

Abundant Storage

Homeowners demand more storage space in their homes. In fact, homes with insufficient storage space soon must give up a room or the garage to storage for belongings. Examples are expanded walk-in closets, built-in storage cabinets, closet-efficiency systems, and storage outbuildings.

Cultural Upgrades

Modern homes are trending toward the application of ideas and philosophies from other cultures. Feng shui (see page 27), for example, is an ancient Chinese philosophy that is being incorporated into the designs of today's homes. *Vastu shastra* is an ancient Indian philosophy that can be applied for harmonious home design. Both are aimed at removing obstructions to positive energies so the energy can flow freely in a living space. In addition, incorporating the best living and housing ideas of other cultures offers a new perspective toward harmonious living.

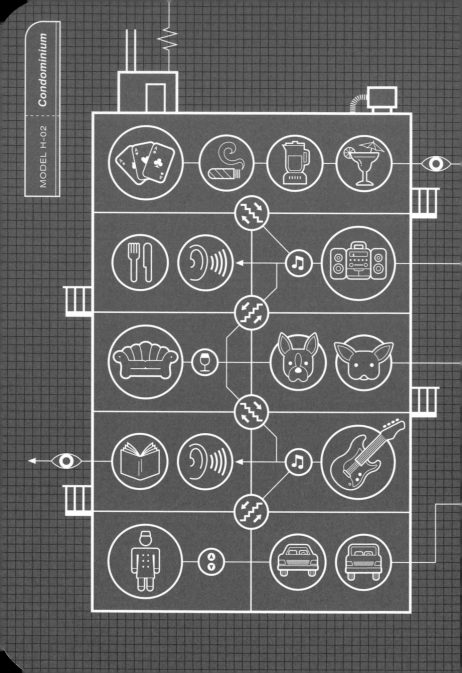

Chapter 2

Installation

Installing Occupants

Installation of most consumer products requires placing the unit in a convenient location and preparing it for use. Because homes are large and already in place, it is the occupants who are installed. This process requires the following steps:

[**1**] Determine occupant requirements.

[**2**] Select the appropriate residence to meet those requirements.

[**3**] Purchase the residence.

[**4**] Move into the residence.

The purpose of this chapter is to present the process, requirements, and options for installing occupants into an appropriate residence.

⚠ *CAUTION: Improper installation of occupants into a residence or installation of occupants into an unsuitable residence may cause damage to persons, relationships, or mental health. For best results, carefully follow appropriate instructions.*

Determining Occupant Requirements

To determine the best application of occupants to residences, consider the requirements of the occupants as a group as well as individual inhabitants. Analyze specific needs for type, usage, location, and condition of the residential candidate. Each candidate was designed and built to fulfill specific requirements for potential occupants. Successfully matching occupants to a residence ensures optimum performance of both.

Selecting by Type

There are four primary types of residences (see page 29–30), which can be grouped into three functional categories:

Single-Family Residence (SFR) houses offer separation from neighbors, often with a yard area (page 44).

Planned-Unit Developments (PUDs) or townhouses share walls with neighbors, but offer exterior doors (page 45).

Condominiums (condos) or co-op apartments share walls with neighbors, with ingress and egress to common hallways (pages 46–47).

The variables are unit access and proximity to neighbors. Within each type of home, there are variations that blur the lines of separation. For example, some SFRs are built on lots so small that neighboring doors are within just a few feet of each other. Other homes are constructed on large lots or even acreage that limit the view of a neighbor's door.

If given the option, many occupants would prefer residences with the greatest privacy: a large home on at least 20 acres of land. However, costs typically are prohibitive in most locations, so occupants compromise on

(Fig. A)
SINGLE-FAMILY RESIDENCE

(Fig. B)
PLANNED-UNIT DEVELOPMENT

RESIDENCE TYPES: Single-family homes and planned-unit developments offer easy acess to street level.

(Fig. C)
CONDOMINIUM

RESIDENCE TYPES: In urban environments, condominiums are often stacked in a vertical formation.

various elements, including proximity to neighbors, and opt to implement other privacy measures. Occupants who were raised in congested areas often are more willing to make this compromise than those who were not.

Determining Usage

Approximately six million owner-occupant installations are made each year in the United States into homes ranging in size from 600 sq ft (55.7 sq m) cabins to 6,000 sq ft (557.4 sq m) estate homes. The typical installation is into a 2,300 sq ft (214 sq m) residence with three bedrooms, two bathrooms, and other functional areas or rooms.

Space within a home can be functionally categorized as:

 Communal: Family, visitors

 Service: Kitchen, baths, laundry

 Private: Bedrooms, leisure

 Work: Home office, garage shop

 Circulation: Entryway, hallways, stairs

 EXPERT TIP: *When analyzing housing requirements, separate* needs *from* wants. *The family unit may* want *a fully equipped media center but only* needs *cable service to a corner of the living room and a bedroom. A residence must meet all of the needs—including financial—of the family unit before it considers the wants.*

To establish functional and space requirements of occupants, analyze the various requirements of individuals then of the group. Following are questions to assist in determining housing space requirements:

- Is a formal or casual home preferred?
- How many bedrooms are currently required?
- How large must the primary or master bedroom be?
- Do any bedrooms require a walk-in closet?
- How long will younger occupants be living at home, and what are their short-term bedroom requirements? Long-term requirements?
- How many bathrooms are needed? Closest to which rooms? Tub, shower, both, or neither?
- Does the family unit prefer a large living/great room for unity or a smaller living room and a game/media room for separation?
- What kitchen components best fit the family unit's lifestyle?
- Is a separate laundry room important? If so, should it be near the living area for convenience or in the basement or garage for space?
- Are TV, music, and games important enough to the family unit to *require* a separate media room?
- How many cars will need to be garaged? Attached or detached?
- How much storage space will the family unit require?
- How important is privacy to installed occupants? Security? Community?
- How much time do family unit members currently spend at home? In what part of the house? Doing what?
- How would family unit members *like* to spend time at a new home?
- What are the most efficient and cost-effective home comfort systems in the area?

Finally, consider future usage of the home. What changes in the family can be anticipated? Will supplementary room be needed for additional children? Will older children be moving out soon? Will maturing children require additional privacy? A well-selected residence can respond to anticipated changes without being replaced.

Choosing a Location

Because homes are considered immovable, location is important. In fact, the cost of a home is highly dependent upon its location, specifically its proximity to employment centers, commercial services, and leisure opportunities. Otherwise, smart homebuyers would select a lower-priced Midwest home and move it to one of the more-expensive coastal areas.

The three primary factors in selecting a residential location are convenience, neighborhood, and investment potential.

Convenience: Make sure that the home selected is as convenient as possible to work sites. Complexity comes from a family unit having multiple work sites that must be considered along with proximity to specific schools (short- and long-term), and other off-site obligations.

⚠ **EXPERT TIP:** *When searching for a home location, mark a local map with the location of existing obligations (work, school, social) for all family unit members. Add to it locations that may vary because of work or school changes. Identify the primary obligations in red. Mark the primary roads near these obligations in blue. This exercise helps in identifying primary location candidates for further research.*

Neighborhood: A neighborhood is a group of residences that share commonalities. Some are identified by the initial development name, such as *Brooktrails*. Others are named for the location of homes similar in pricing and available services, for example *Southeast*. Whether new or established, these neighborhoods share features and benefits that may or may not fit a specific home-occupant candidate's requirements.

⚠ **EXPERT TIP:** *To determine the personality of candidate neighborhoods, ask residents, real estate agents, lenders, and area businesspeople to help identify the area's characteristics. Ask what they like and dislike about the area. Also check area newspapers for real estate ads that may help identify and characterize specific neighborhoods under consideration. Finally, drive or walk through the candidate neighborhoods for an on-site assessment of their personalities.*

Investment Potential: Depending on the planned length of ownership in a neighborhood, the investment potential of residences can be critical. For example, moving into a neighborhood that clearly is ebbing may not be a good investment unless held for ten or more years. Nor is moving into a neighborhood where housing prices are artificially inflated. Like selecting stocks, selecting a profitable home requires research. Unlike stocks, a poor investment cannot be quickly sold.

⚠ **EXPERT TIP:** *The best source for historical sales data for homes is a local real estate appraiser. Alternatively, an experienced real estate salesperson may offer tips on housing trends specific to neighborhoods. Appraisers charge a fee and salespeople do not. You often get what you pay for.*

Analyzing Condition

The condition of a home also is an important component of the decision to buy. Condition not only dictates the livability of the structure, but also the value and the work that may be required to make it livable and comfortable to the family unit.

Home condition can be categorized as new, pre-owned, or distressed. New, obviously, requires no repairs to be livable; decorating to taste may be all that is necessary before moving in. Pre-owned condition shows some wear but requires no major (over $1,000) repairs. A distressed home will require major repairs to make it habitable. The price of a selected home should reflect its condition and the costs of making needed repairs and remodeling.

⚠ *CAUTION: The Universal Remodeling Rule (URR) states that all projects take more time and more money than budgeted.*

New Homes

Nearly 1.5 million new homes are built in the United States annually, about 10 percent by the owners, 15 percent by contractors for the owners, and 75 percent for sale to the highest bidder. Advantage: All components are new, unused, and ready for personalization. Disadvantage: Cost of personalizing a home and lot can add thousands of dollars to the total purchase price.

Pre-Owned Homes

The majority of occupied homes are pre-owned, some with histories of 100 years or more and numerous families and remodeling projects. Advantage: Homes are established and in established neighborhoods. Disadvantage: Because components are of varying age and condition, maintenance and repair can bring unexpected expenses.

Distressed Homes

Some habitable homes are riddled with deferred maintenance projects that require remedies before they can be livable. Advantage: Initial cost of ownership typically is low and, if problems are corrected, resale value can be high. Disadvantage: Initial savings may be eaten up by needed repair projects, especially if professional assistance is required.

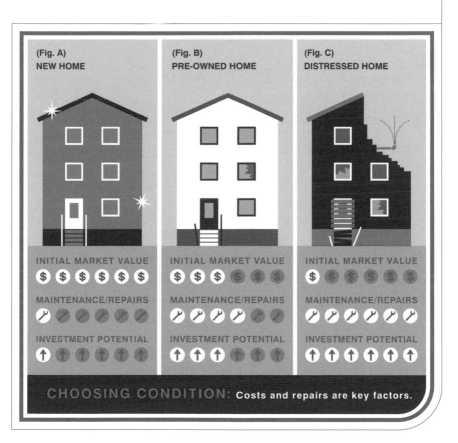

Home Pre-Acquisition Inspection

Once the family unit's requirements are identified (see page 48), potential
tion Checklist. Determine which components are most important to the family

AREA	CHECK FOR	CONDITION			
		Excellent	Good	Fair	Poor
Attic	Accessibility	O	O	O	O
	Construction	O	O	O	O
	Insulation	O	O	O	O
	Leaks	O	O	O	O
	Ventilation	O	O	O	O
Basement	Columns	O	O	O	O
	Foundation walls	O	O	O	O
	Girders	O	O	O	O
	Joists	O	O	O	O
	Mold	O	O	O	O
	Water seepage	O	O	O	O
Crawl Space (below main floor)	Construction	O	O	O	O
	Floor	O	O	O	O
	Insulation	O	O	O	O
	Leaks	O	O	O	O
	Pests	O	O	O	O
	Termites	O	O	O	O
	Ventilation	O	O	O	O
Electrical System	Breakers	O	O	O	O
	Fixtures	O	O	O	O

Checklist

purchasers can inspect home candidates using a Home Pre-Acquisition Inspec-
unit and rate them for functionality and relative condition for each property.

AREA	CHECK FOR	CONDITION			
		Excellent	Good	Fair	Poor
Electrical System *(continued)*	Fuses	○	○	○	○
	Ground buss	○	○	○	○
	Outlets	○	○	○	○
	Service panel	○	○	○	○
	Switches	○	○	○	○
	Wiring	○	○	○	○
Exterior	Caulking	○	○	○	○
	Chimney	○	○	○	○
	Deck	○	○	○	○
	Doors	○	○	○	○
	Drainage	○	○	○	○
	Driveway	○	○	○	○
	Fence	○	○	○	○
	Garage	○	○	○	○
	Gutters and downspouts	○	○	○	○
	Landscaping	○	○	○	○
	Patio	○	○	○	○
	Porch	○	○	○	○
	Roof	○	○	○	○
	Screens	○	○	○	○

AREA	CHECK FOR	CONDITION			
		Excellent	Good	Fair	Poor
Exterior *(continued)*	**Steps**	O	O	O	O
	Termites	O	O	O	O
	Trim	O	O	O	O
	Walks	O	O	O	O
	Walls	O	O	O	O
	Windows	O	O	O	O
Heating and Cooling	**Connections**	O	O	O	O
	Controls	O	O	O	O
	Distribution system	O	O	O	O
	Fireplace	O	O	O	O
	Fuel source	O	O	O	O
	Furnace	O	O	O	O
	Air conditioner	O	O	O	O
	Insulation	O	O	O	O
	Motors and fans	O	O	O	O
	Ventilation	O	O	O	O
Hot Water System	**Capacity**	O	O	O	O
	Condition	O	O	O	O
	Fuel source	O	O	O	O
	Recovery	O	O	O	O
	Relief valve	O	O	O	O
	Tank or tankless	O	O	O	O
Plumbing System	**Drain condition**	O	O	O	O
	Drain lines	O	O	O	O

AREA	CHECK FOR	CONDITION			
		Excellent	Good	Fair	Poor
Plumbing System *(continued)*	**Fixtures**	○	○	○	○
	Pipe materials	○	○	○	○
	Septic tank and lines	○	○	○	○
	Sewer lines	○	○	○	○
	Shutoff	○	○	○	○
	Water pressure	○	○	○	○
	Well and storage	○	○	○	○
Rooms **(check each)**	**Cabinets**	○	○	○	○
	Ceiling	○	○	○	○
	Closets	○	○	○	○
	Countertops	○	○	○	○
	Doors	○	○	○	○
	Electrical outlets	○	○	○	○
	Electrical switches	○	○	○	○
	Exhaust fan	○	○	○	○
	Floor	○	○	○	○
	Hardware	○	○	○	○
	Heating	○	○	○	○
	Insulation	○	○	○	○
	Plumbing fixtures	○	○	○	○
	Trim	○	○	○	○
	Ventilation	○	○	○	○
	Walls	○	○	○	○
	Windows	○	○	○	○

Shopping for a Home

The selection process for a housing unit can be a daunting task, especially for consumers who have no prior experience. Fortunately, the task is well documented. More than 16,000 U.S. homes are purchased *each day*.

Using Agents

About 85 percent of housing units are purchased with the assistance of real estate agents. A real estate agent is a state-licensed broker or salesperson who is legally authorized to manage real estate transactions *for a fee*.

EXPERT TIP: Not all real estate agents are Realtors®, who also are members of the National Association of Realtors (NAR). Membership does not guarantee professionalism, but may indicate a professional attitude toward real estate transactions.

The fee typically is based on the final sale price of the property sold. Though real estate fees are negotiable and cannot be set by law, most real estate agents charge about six percent for transactions involving homes and about 10 percent for those of vacant land. Local competition or lack of it may dictate higher or lower fees. The real estate fee for selling a $250,000 home, for example, typically is $15,000.

Because most real estate transactions include more than one broker or salesperson, the fee or commission is split among the parties. The listing office typically gets half and the selling office gets the other half, though local market conditions may dictate a different split. Each office has a real estate broker and numerous licensed salespeople. Experienced salespeople will get half of the office's part of the fee. In this example, the salesperson who assists the buyer in purchasing a $250,000 home will receive about $3,750 in fees if and when the property actually transfers ownership. The actual split is not relevant to the home buyer, but does indicate the level of payment a successful real estate salesperson will receive for finding a buyer for a home.

In most residential real estate transactions, it is the home's seller who actually pays the real estate fee—though the fee typically is built into the asking price. In fact, the real estate broker and office usually are hired and paid by the seller rather than the buyer. This is an important fact because it means that *all* real estate agents within the transaction are legally obligated to work on the behalf of the *seller* rather than the buyer. Of course, without the buyer there is no transaction.

EXPERT TIP: Make sure you ask your real estate agent to explain state laws regarding agency and who has what responsibilities within a real estate transaction. How professionally the agent answers this question can be as telling as what is said.

Selecting a suitable real estate agent can be daunting. Many home buyers choose whichever agent is most prominent on For Sale signs within the selected neighborhood. Others use a friend or relative who sells real estate in the area. The best choice is whoever best understands the local real estate market and attempts to understand the family unit's housing requirements. A short interview with a real estate agent should quickly reveal the agent's knowledge and attitude.

The advantage to using a real estate agent is the agent's knowledge of real estate law, title issues, transaction requirements, lender options, available residential inventory, and negotiation. The disadvantage is the cost of such skills that is included within the purchase price.

Buying FSBOs

A licensed real estate agent is not a required component in a housing transaction. Legal issues can be resolved by a real estate attorney, and lenders can manage the financial paperwork. This means that home-ownership candidates can purchase directly from a home's owner who is not already contracted to a real estate agent. These homes are referred to as "For Sale by Owner" or FSBOs (pronounced *fizz-boze*).

FSBOs can be found by driving through selected neighborhoods looking for nonagent signs on candidate properties. In addition, owners typically place classified ads in the real estate section of area news-papers. Buyers also read local real estate publications or search the Internet for FSBOs.

EXPERT TIP: *Not all professional real estate signs are placed on homes by licensed agents. Some signs are provided by FSBO services (for a fee) that assist owners in marketing their homes to buyers without a real estate agent.*

The advantage to buying directly from the owner is a potentially lower cost because real estate sales fees typically aren't included in the price. The disadvantage is that the buyer is required to do more of the research and leg-work than if an agent is hired to manage the trans-action. In addition, a buyer without negotiating skills may lose thou-sands of dollars to an experienced seller.

EXPERT TIP: *If you've found a FSBO that you like but prefer to use a real estate agent, ask the owner if they will pay an agency fee. Many will. In addition, most agents will reduce their fee if a ready-made transaction is brought to them.*

Closing on a Home

The home-buying process can seem complex. In many transactions, it is. However, the process of transferring title to a residential property is as easy as one, two, three.

[**1**] Seller and buyer agree to the terms of the transaction.

[**2**] Title and money are simultaneously transferred between seller and buyer.

[**3**] Buyer takes possession of the property.

The complexity is in the detailed tasks required in the transaction process. Fortunately, there are professional services available that will manage many of the details of a real estate transaction. The primary one is called an *escrow service*. An escrow is a disinterested third party who follows the instructions agreed upon by the seller and buyer in the Purchase and Sale Agreement. The agreement includes the transaction terms *in writing*:

- Final purchase price and how it will be paid
- Legal description of the property and what rights are being transferred
- Conditions (contingencies) for financing, inspection, appraisals, and other transfer steps
- Who pays for what services (title insurance, escrow, inspections, financing)

EXPERT TIP: A title search identifies all owners, lenders, and lien-holders on the property. Title insurance is a service that guarantees that the seller has legal rights to transfer title to the subject property. In most transactions, title search and insurance services are paid for by the seller.

If there are real estate agents involved in the transaction, there will be clauses in the agreement to protect them and to pay them.

Escrow services can be provided by the primary lender, the title company, an attorney, or an escrow service business. Seller and buyer must agree on which service provider to use and who pays the fees. In most transactions, the escrow costs are split between buyer and seller.

Paying for a Home

Residential real estate often is the largest transaction most individuals make. The majority of homes are purchased with the assistance of lenders who invest in the homeowner's ability to repay the debt. If unpaid, the home becomes the lender's property.

Cash Talks

Though the majority of home transactions require lenders, most home sales are for "cash." Actually, it's "cash, subject to securing a loan" or "cash to the seller." Because most sellers receive cash for their equity (sale price less transaction costs less what they owe a lender), there is little negotiating advantage to the buyer for offering "all cash" for a home. The single advantage is that an all-cash transaction may close much faster because the buyer doesn't have to apply and wait for financing on the property. Depending on the seller's need to sell, an all-cash transaction with no lender involved gives the buyer a slight negotiating advantage.

Conventional Financing

For most home transactions, financing is required. If the funds come from a mortgage lender, the financing is considered conventional. The buyer provides a portion of the transaction price, called the *down payment*, and the lender furnishes the rest.

Because most homes are good financial investments, most buyers contribute the smallest amount they can to the transaction. Because lenders want to ensure that the buyer is committed to making payments, they prefer the largest down payment the buyer can provide and will charge higher interest rates for greater risk.

EXPERT TIP: *Most housing lenders use the same loan application to make the decision process easier. It's called the URLA or Uniform Residential Loan Application. Pick one up from any lender and begin studying it; a complete and accurate application can make the lending process go easier.*

EXPERT TIP: *Many lenders use the 28/36 qualifying ratio. The total monthly payment (principal, interest, taxes, insurance, or PITI) must be less than 28 percent and total debts must be less than 36 percent of the total household income. If you will have no debts except the house (cars paid off, etc.), the maximum PITI is 36 percent of income.*

The typical down payment on most homes today is 10 to 20 percent. Lenders prefer that buyers provide at least 20 percent of the home's selling price and will require the buyer to pay private mortgage insurance (PMI) if less than 20 percent is put down. The Veterans Administration (VA) and some Housing and Urban Development (HUD) loans may pay the PMI for qualified buyers who have smaller or even no down payment.

⚗ **EXPERT TIP:** *Start shopping for a mortgage with your current banker as you may get preferential treatment or rates. You also will get an education in how mortgages and lenders work.*

Unconventional Financing

For various reasons, including poor credit, many home buyers choose non-standard or unconventional financing. Because lenders typically are taking greater risk, the rates often are higher than with conventional financing.

The most popular type of unconventional financing is buying on a real estate contract held by the seller. The advantage to the seller is that the interest rate paid may be higher than what the seller would get by investing the sale's proceeds in a savings account, certificate of deposit, or other asset. The advantage to the buyer is less-stringent credit requirements and, in some cases, a lower down payment than available from conventional financing. Real estate contract financing is popular with many cooperative apartment sales. The seller is also the lender.

Moving In

A residential property legally transfers ownership when the transaction is filed and recorded at the county courthouse. Once recorded, the escrow company will disburse payments to the seller, any real estate agents, and to other services in the transaction as directed by the Purchase and Sale Agreement and the financial documents called *closing papers*. Until that point, it is the seller's property, and the buyer cannot occupy it unless an agreement otherwise has been made *in writing*.

The next challenge for homebuyers is moving in. Several options are available.

Moving Companies

Most local moving companies are agents of a larger network of moving services. The local service will pack belongings and move them within the area or prepare the belongings for pick-up by a regional or national truck for long-distance moving.

The process of using a moving company is as follows:

[1] Contact the local moving service for an estimate appointment.

[2] Review the estimate of costs and sign the moving order.

[3] Prepare for packing day.

[4] Prepare for unpacking day.

Depending on the length of time required for the home-buying trans-action and the proximity of the current and purchased homes, most moving companies prefer two to four weeks' advance notice. More is better. Less is more expensive. In busier moving times, such as the summer, allow a few extra weeks, because packing and moving crews may be busy. If necessary, belongings can be packed early for storage then moved when the new home unit is available.

Self Moves

First-time home buyers who are moving from apartments may opt for self moves, hiring a rental truck and gathering an amateur moving crew. The advantage is lower cost. The disadvantage is potential damage by inexperienced movers.

Rental moving trucks, trailers, and supplies are available through private companies. Be aware that seemingly low rental charges often do not include mileage fees. Most rental companies also sell boxes and other packing materials.

The process of a self move is as follows:

[**1**] Get rid of all belongings that are not worth moving.

[**2**] Itemize and estimate the size of what will be moved in cubic feet or cubic centimeters.

[**3**] Purchase packing supplies as needed, making sure that unused materials are returnable.

[**4**] Pack and gather all components to be moved.

[**5**] Select the appropriate vehicle for the move, weighing multiple trips against mileage fees.

[**6**] Gather the moving crew, as needed.

[**7**] Move out of the old home, and move to the new one.

[**8**] Move in and unpack.

Component Services

Larger communities have component moving services that provide packing, transporting, unpacking, and other assistance. Check local telephone book business pages under Moving Services for options. For long-distance moves, some services provide moving trailers that the customer packs for transport by a trucking company. All services balance cost and effort.

Moving On

Physically moving into a new residence typically requires emotional adjustments as well. Especially when younger family-unit members are moved, the process can produce unseen problems. Make sure that all group members adequately adjust to the emotional move as well as the physical move. Join local service, social, and spiritual groups as soon as possible.

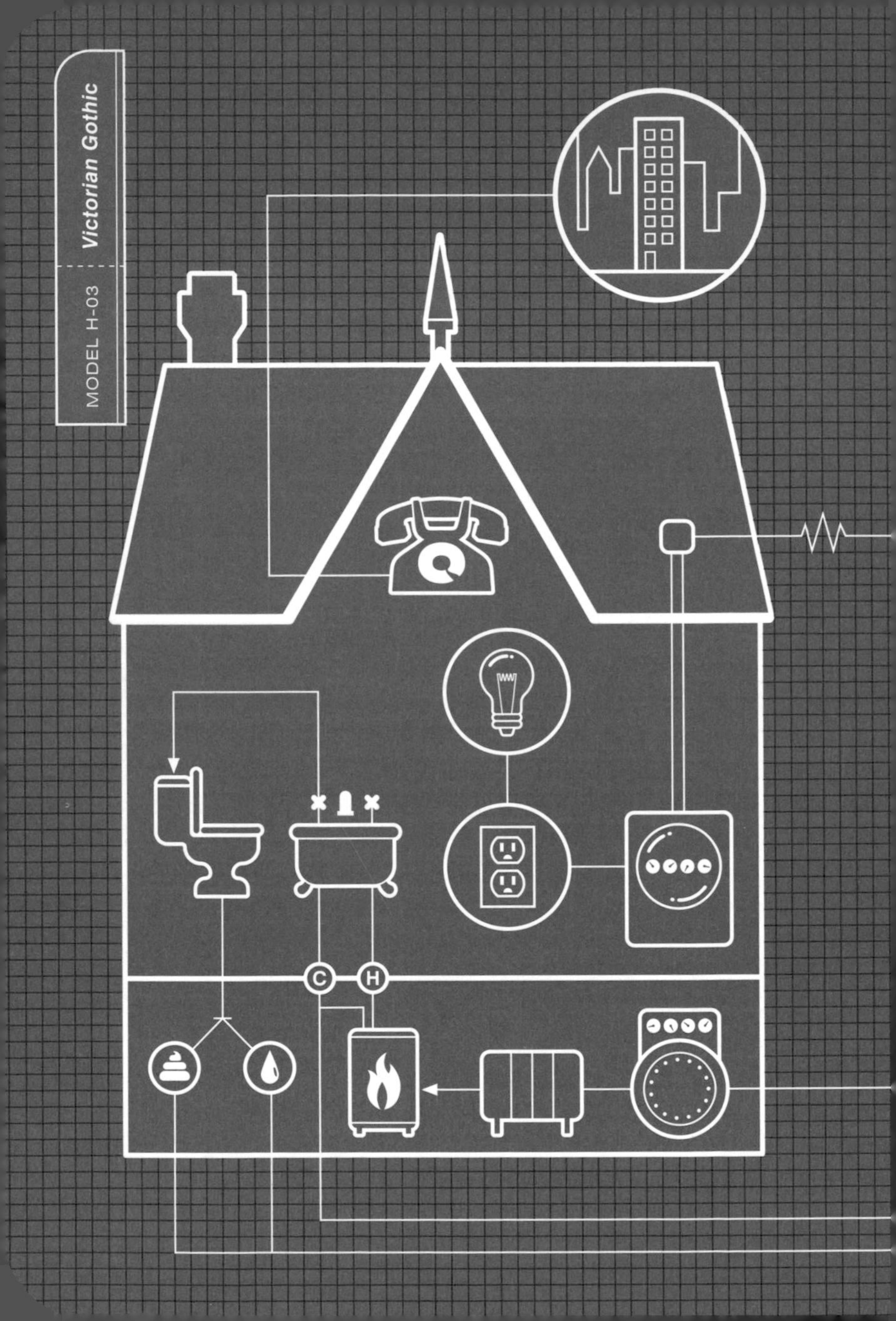
Victorian Gothic
MODEL H-03
C
H

Parts and Service

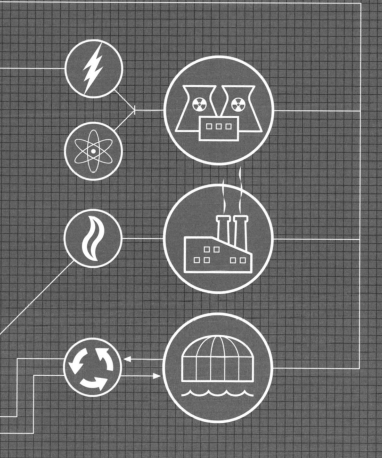

Shelter Requirements

The primary function of a residential housing unit is to shelter occupants. The secondary function is to provide space and energy for devices that support and enhance life. All homes have identical functions, therefore parts and services are standardized. The parts and services in the typical home include structural, electrical, plumbing, heating, and cooling (see pages 15–20). Tools, materials, and safety also are important to the homeowner.

Structural

The structural parts of a home are the components that provide shelter. These components include foundations, floors, stairs, walls, ceilings, and roofs. Secondary components include doors and windows.

Foundations

A home's foundation is the supporting portion below the first floor. It includes the footing that firmly attaches the foundation to the ground as well as the foundation walls that support the floor and other structural components above. Most home foundations are made of concrete that includes reinforcement bar called *rebar*. The foundation evenly distributes the home's weight for stability.

Many homes include space under the residence for ventilation and to provide space for electrical, plumbing, and other service systems. If the space is sufficient for a person to stand, it is called a *basement*, otherwise it is known as a *crawl space*. Some housing units built on sloping land have both a partial basement and a crawl space. If the basement has a finished floor and walls, it is a finished basement. Because heat rises, many homes are built with heating systems within the basement or crawl space area.

Floors

A floor is the horizontal surface that forms the base for levels or stories in a residence. Most home floors include three layers: framing, subfloor, and flooring. The first floor's framing sits atop the foundation and is built from wood members called *joists* fastened together with nails and metal plates. Floor framing evenly distributes the home's weight to the foundation. The subfloor is the horizontal surface of wood or composite products. Flooring materials such as carpet, hardwood, hard tile, or resilient tile are installed on top of the subfloor.

The flooring surface can be changed by the owner or by professional installers. Flooring typically lasts ten to 20 years, depending on type, quality, and use. Some flooring surfaces, such as solid hardwood, can be periodically refinished. Carpets are more absorbent than other materials and usually require more thorough cleaning (see page 94).

Stairs

Stairways are a series of steps connecting one floor to another. A stair step includes the horizontal tread and vertical riser. Three or more risers are called *stairs* or a *stairway*. Stairways are standardized in height, width, and depth to make it easier for occupants to smoothly transition between floors.

Most interior stairways include framing, subfloor, and flooring. Outdoor stairways don't include a flooring material on top of the steps.

Walls

A wall is a vertical structure that encloses, divides, and supports a building or a room. If the wall supports weight from a higher component it is load-bearing, otherwise it is a nonbearing wall. The important difference to the homeowner is that a nonbearing wall can be moved or removed more easily when remodeling.

The components of a wall include the frame and the sheathing, or covering. The frame is made up of vertical members called *studs* and horizontal members known as *top and bottom plates*. Wall studs typically are spaced 16 in (40.6 cm) from center to center, or on-center (oc). Nonbearing walls in some homes may have studs spaced 24 in (61 cm) oc. Knowing the approximate location and spacing of wall studs is important when hanging pictures or heavier objects on walls.

The sheathing or wall covering on newer homes typically is wallboard, also known as drywall, a flat material made up of dry gypsum plaster sandwiched between two sheets of heavy paper. Wallboard is produced in 4-ft (1.2 m) widths in lengths of 8, 10, and 12 ft (2.4, 3, and 3.6 m). The larger sizes are heavier and are used by professional wallboard installers, called *drywallers*. The longest edges are slightly tapered so they can be smoothly joined using drywall tape and wet gypsum plaster.

Older homes may have walls built of lath and plaster. Lath is strips of thin wood that is nailed directly to wall studs with space between the laths. Wet gypsum plaster is then spread over the lath, filling the space between them to adhere. A second coat is spread for a smooth wall surface. Installing lath and plaster requires more skill and effort than installing wallboard, so older homes that are remodeled typically replace lath-and-plaster walls. Homeowners should know how to make simple repairs to both types of wall surfaces (see page 99).

EXPERT TIP: *Damage to walls is easy to repair using wall patch kits and products available from hardware stores.*

Before wall sheathing is installed, homebuilders install other system components, including electrical wiring and fixtures, plumbing pipes, and comfort system ducting (see page 80) through the wall studs.

Doors and Windows

A door is a hinged or sliding component that allows occupants to pass through a wall. Exterior doors typically are large and solid. Interior doors are smaller and less solid, sometimes hollow. Door hardware facilitates or prevents the opening and closing of the door. Because doors are simple components, they can easily be maintained by homeowners (see page 132).

A window is a wall opening that permits the passage and control of light and air into a room. Double-hung windows have a stationary top and sliding bottom half. Casement windows have one section that swings outward. Window glass on some models can be replaced by the homeowner.

Ceilings

Ceilings are horizontal walls. They include a frame and sheathing. The frame is similar to that of a floor and thicker than a wall frame, as it must support the roof or higher stories. The sheathing is similar to that of walls, typically of wallboard or lath and plaster, though thicker to minimize sag. Before the sheathing is installed, builders mount electrical, plumbing, and comfort system components within them.

Roofs

A home's roof is its outside top covering. Depending on local climate conditions and whether heavy rain or snow may accumulate on the roof surface, the roof is constructed with a specific pitch (angle). Roof components include a frame, sheathing, and roofing. The frame is made up of wood members with various names depending on their functions. The sheathing typically is sheets of plywood or other material that covers the frame. Finally, the roofing material is applied, often with a protective moisture barrier between the material and the sheathing.

⚠ **EXPERT TIP:** *The most common damage to roofs is caused by blocked gutters and downspouts that allow water or ice to lift roof tiles and enter the home.*

Water runoff from the roof is caught by gutters and distributed to the ground or in-ground wells through downspouts. As there are no moving parts, maintenance and repairs are minimal.

Electrical

Electrical systems distribute electricity throughout the home. The major components include the electrical service panel, circuit breakers and fuses, wiring, switches, fixtures, and outlets.

The electrical service panel is the point of entry for electricity into the home. Overhead or underground wires from the power company connect to the meter that measures the home's electric usage. Once measured, the incoming electricity is delivered to the adjacent electrical service panel, where it begins the distribution process to specific circuits within the home. Most modern homes have 20 to 30 circuits. Each circuit may serve one or more outlets (plugs) or fixtures.

A fixture is a device that uses electricity. A ceiling light, for example, is a fixture. Larger appliances are plugged into a single outlet that is a dedicated circuit with no other devices drawing electricity from it. Other circuits may have multiple outlets that can simultaneously serve numerous electrical appliances and devices.

Electrical circuits are designed with limits. If the combined devices on the circuit draw more electricity than it is designed for, the wiring within the wall may overheat. To prevent this unsafe condition, each circuit has a limiter, either a circuit breaker or a fuse, which stops excessive electricity from passing through the wires. If overworked, circuit breakers "trip," or turn themselves off, and fuses "blow" or melt. Once the problem is solved, the circuit breaker can be reset or the fuse replaced.

⚠️ **EXPERT TIP:** *Every homeowner should own and know how to use a multimeter, also known as a* volt-ohmmeter *(VOM), to test electrical circuits and appliances. Units are available for less than $15 and include directions for safe use.*

The amount of electricity used in a circuit is measured in amperes, or amps. Fixtures and appliances all have markings indicating how many amps they require, or "draw." The limit of a specific circuit is marked on the circuit breaker or fuse. Most household circuits are limited to carrying 15, 20, or 30 amps each. Some circuits with larger equipment, such as a kitchen range, may require higher amperage circuit breakers or fuses.

An important component within each electrical circuit is the controller or switch that turns the circuit ON (closes the circuit) or OFF (opens the circuit). Most switches are two-way (called *single-pole*) switches, meaning the fixture can be turned on or off from one location. Controlling light fixtures from two locations requires a three-way switch. A four-way switch controls the fixture from three locations (3 + OFF = 4), common on hallway light circuits. Dimmer switches allow a circuit to progressively deliver electricity to a light fixture.

Wire is the conduit, or road, for electricity. The larger the wire, the more electricity it can safely carry. However, the *larger* the American Wire Gauge (AWG) number, the *smaller* the wire is. A 10 AWG wire is *larger* than a 16 AWG wire and can safely deliver more electricity. It is also more expensive.

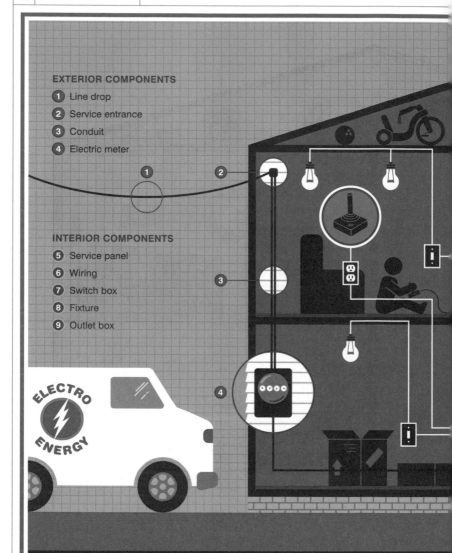

EXTERIOR COMPONENTS

1. Line drop
2. Service entrance
3. Conduit
4. Electric meter

INTERIOR COMPONENTS

5. Service panel
6. Wiring
7. Switch box
8. Fixture
9. Outlet box

ELECTRO ENERGY

ELECTRICAL SYSTEM COMPONENTS: Electricity is distributed

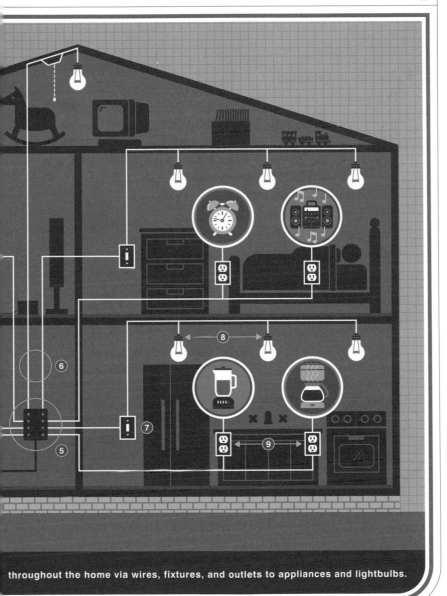

throughout the home via wires, fixtures, and outlets to appliances and lightbulbs.

Finally, an electrical cord plug is inserted into the receptacle or outlet to receive electricity. Newer outlets allow two polarized prongs (of different sizes) and a grounded prong. Plugs for larger appliances and 240 v equipment use various prong configurations to ensure that they are not plugged into the wrong power outlet.

⚠ *CAUTION: Never modify the prongs of an electrical plug to fit into an outlet for which it was not designed.*

Plumbing

Plumbing systems distribute fresh water through the home and remove waste. For health reasons, these two functions are provided by two separate systems: fresh water and drain-waste-vent (DWV).

Fresh water is distributed to homes by a water district or from a private well or spring. If purchased, water first passes through a water meter to measure usage. Between the meter and the house is a shutoff valve that can stop all water from entering the home's plumbing system. The shutoff is useful when repairing a system leak.

Fresh water fixtures control the flow of hot and cold water. Fresh water fixtures typically include a shutoff valve nearby to turn water off to the fixture for repair or replacement.

💡 *EXPERT TIP: To identify whether a water line is hot or cold, carefully touch the line to measure relative temperature. On a faucet, the hot water line typically is on the left.*

There are different types of faucets. If a faucet has two handles that rise when the water is turned on, it is a compression valve faucet. If the

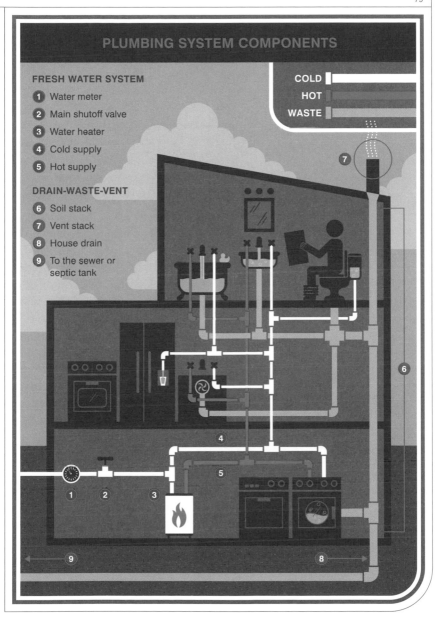

PLUMBING SYSTEM COMPONENTS

FRESH WATER SYSTEM

1. Water meter
2. Main shutoff valve
3. Water heater
4. Cold supply
5. Hot supply

DRAIN-WASTE-VENT

6. Soil stack
7. Vent stack
8. House drain
9. To the sewer or septic tank

COLD
HOT
WASTE

handles lower when water is turned on, it is a reverse-compression valve. If a faucet has only one lever for both hot and cold water, it is a cartridge or ball type. Outdoor faucets usually are cold-water compression types.

Waste lines include a U-shaped trap below the sink, tub, or shower fixture to keep sewer gases and their odors out of the home. Toilets have built-in traps. DWV systems also have vent lines to vent sewer gases to above the home's roof, where they dissipate. Waste lines include a cleanout that can be removed to clean out debris if necessary, normally outside of the home's foundation.

Heating

Home heating systems include a heat source and a distribution system. The more temperate the climate, the simpler the heating system.

Primary heating source types include coal furnace, electric furnace, gas furnace, oil furnace, wood furnace or fireplace, heat pump, electric radiant, and solar. Some heat sources directly heat the home's air while others transfer heat to a liquid, such as water, or other mass that heats the air. Greater efficiency comes from the selection and maintenance of the heater unit.

Home heat is distributed naturally by the movement of warm air, by fans, or by a forced-air distribution system that disperses it through large pipes called *ducts*. Forced-air systems with fans typically include a return system that pulls cool air back to the heat source for reheating. Forced-air systems include a filter to trap large airborne particles. Some distribution systems include electronic ionization filters to trap smaller particles.

Major components of the home heating source include a fuel burner and associated controls. Fuel (gas or oil) is distributed to the burner by

HEATING AND COOLING SYSTEMS

(Fig. A)
HEATING SYSTEM COMPONENTS

1 Heating source
2 Blower
3 Plenum
4 Vents
5 Return-air duct

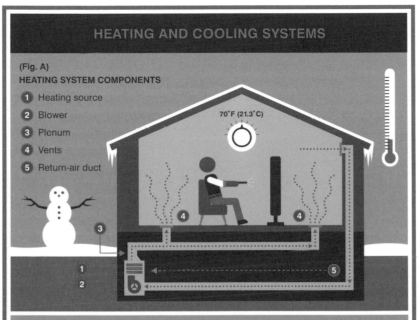

(Fig. B)
COOLING SYSTEM COMPONENTS

1 Air conditioner
2 Refrigerant lines
3 Blower
4 Plenum
5 Vents
6 Return-air duct

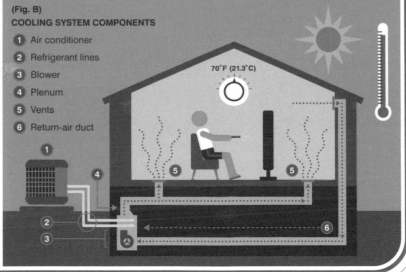

the controller or manually by the operator. The controller measures the ambient temperature and matches it against the control temperature set by the operator. If the ambient temperature is lower, it feeds more fuel to the burner. If the ambient temperature is at or higher than the control temperature, the controller stops fuel from flowing to the burner.

Most heating system repairs require trained technicians. However, homeowners can perform most heating system maintenance functions following step-by-step procedures (see pages 110–118).

Cooling

Home cooling systems include a cooling source and a distribution system. Cool air is distributed naturally by the movement of cooler air, by fans, or by forced-air distribution systems that also distribute heated air at other times.

Primary cooling sources include air conditioners, evaporation coolers, and heat pumps. Air conditioners are refrigeration units that draw warmer room air over cooler coils. Evaporation coolers draw air through a water mist to cool and moisturize the air. A heat pump cools air by removing heat from it.

The components of a home cooling system include the cooler and associated controls. Most home cooling system repairs require trained technicians. However, homeowners can perform most cooling system maintenance functions following step-by-step procedures (see pages 110–118).

EXPERT TIP: *The most common problem facing home cooling units is blockage to cooling fins caused by dirty filters or varmints.*

Security

To maintain the security of occupants, homes have security devices and even full security systems.

A security system is a set of electric sensors designed to trigger an alarm if someone attempts to gain unauthorized access to a home. Security sensors placed at strategic locations on a residence continually check status and report results to the central control unit. The control unit tracks status of all sensors and, if it recognizes an unsecure condition, activates an audible alarm and/or an automatic telephone dialer to summon help.

EXPERT TIP: Newer security systems include sensitivity settings that allow homeowners to minimize false alarms. Follow the alarm's owner's manual for specific information.

Other home security components include locks and latches at doors and windows. A lock is a door fastener operated by a key or knob. A latch is a device that holds a door or window closed. Exterior doors often have both a key-in-knob lock and a deadbolt or rim lock. Simple maintenance procedures (see page 95) can keep home locks and latches operating securely for many years.

Benefits of Maintenance

Home repairs are required when damage has been done to one of the systems. Because most home components are designed to operate smoothly *if properly maintained*, the key to minimizing costly and time-consuming repairs is to maintain home systems. Chapter 6 will cover common emergency repairs. More important, Chapters 4 and 5 outline common interior and exterior maintenance procedures that any home-owner can perform. All of the basic tools and materials needed to perform these maintenance tasks are available at local hardware stores and home centers.

Maintenance Materials

Structural

Lumber is wood cut to a specific size. In the United States, a board is lumber that is more than 2 in wide and less than 2 in thick. Dimension lumber is 2–5 in thick. Timber is more than 5 in thick. Lumber sizes are expressed in their nominal size before being smoothed or planed. For example, a 2 x 4 in stud actually measures $1^5/_8$ x $3^5/_8$, but is referred to as a two-by-four.

Wallboard is available in 4 ft widths and lengths of 8, 10, or 12 ft, depending on the application. Thinner $^1/_4$-in wallboard is used as a backing to wall paneling. The $^1/_2$-in size is common for walls that will be painted. Ceilings are usually built with $^5/_8$-in wallboard. Wallboard is also known as *drywall*, *plasterboard*, and *gypsum wallboard* (GWB).

EXPERT TIP: *Damage to wallboard can be fixed using patch kits that include fabric and patch plaster available at hardware stores. Smaller dings to walls can be repaired with patch plaster (see page 99).*

Most homeowners won't have to replace lumber or wallboard in their home, but may make repairs and should know what is available.

Electrical

Electrical system components purchased by homeowners include replacement circuit breakers, fuses, switches, outlets, and fixtures.

⚠ *CAUTION: Make sure that the electrical circuit being worked on is turned off at the service panel before starting any repairs or replacement.*

Electrical components are labeled for amperage (amps). Circuit breakers and fuses are clearly labeled in amps (A) and must be replaced with one of equal amperage. Outlets and switches are often available in boxes with installation instructions included (see page 100). Homeowners should take an old fixture to the hardware store to find an exact replacement.

Replacement fixtures, such as lights and fans, are more complex to select and install. However, most units include printed instructions that can be read at the store before purchasing.

Plumbing

Plumbing systems (see page 78) consist of pipes and fixtures. Fresh water pipes are 1 in (25.4 mm) or less in diameter. DWV pipes are $1^{1}/_{2}$ to 3 in (38.1–76.2 mm) in diameter, so they are relatively easy to differentiate. Fresh water pipe materials include brass, copper, galvanized steel, and plastic (polyvinyl chloride, or PVC). DWV materials include cast iron and black PVC.

Plumbing fixtures include toilets, bidets, sinks, tubs, showers, and faucets. Fixtures are standardized to common sizes that make replacement easier. Homeowners should make sure they have the exact dimension of any component to be replaced. If possible, bring smaller fixtures or the original installation manual to the retailer when purchasing replacements.

⚠ **EXPERT TIP:** *When buying replacement fixtures, retain the packing material and all literature in case it is the incorrect unit and must be returned for credit.*

Heating and Cooling

Heating and cooling systems usually are not repaired by homeowners, though regular maintenance can minimize repairs. The primary component that needs maintenance in heating and cooling systems is the filter. Using the owner's manuals or an inspection, homeowners should identify the make and model of all heating and cooling appliances within the home. In most cases, they are identified on a metal plate or label on the main component. The filter will typically be located on the outlet side of the appliance. Filters that don't have part numbers on them can be removed and taken to a hardware store for an exact replacement.

Selecting and Using Tools and Fasteners

A tool is an implement that drives, cuts, turns, grabs, or attaches materials, fixtures, or fasteners. Basic tools for the homeowner's tool kit should include the following:

Basic homeowner's tool kit

- An 8- or 16-ounce (225–450 g) hammer for installing and removing nails
- An adjustable wrench for tightening and loosening bolts
- A screwdriver with assorted tips for tightening and loosening screws
- Adjustable pliers for holding or turning things
- A multimeter, or volt-ohmmeter, for testing electrical voltage, current, and resistance

Including a small plastic toolbox, the basic homeowner's toolkit should cost less than $25. Double that amount to add:

- Wire strippers for cutting and removing the outer wrapper or insulation from around wires.
- Retractable-blade utility knife for cutting softer materials
- 10-ft (3-m) measuring tape.
- Plastic paint tray, roller, cover, handle, and brushes

Most homeowners continue to expand their tool kits with more specialized tools as needs warrant. However, most will use at least one of the above for home maintenance and repair jobs for many years.

⚠ **EXPERT TIP:** *Spend a little more and get better quality tools. If you need assistance, ask a hardware store clerk for recommendations based on your budget and comfort level. A tool designed for a specific job can make the job much easier to complete.*

Fasteners attach two or more materials. Fasteners include nails, screws, bolts, and adhesives. Nails are thin, pointed, metal fasteners that are driven with a hammer to join two pieces of wood. Common nails have larger heads than finish nails. The size of nails is indicated as *penny* (abbreviated *d*) relative to their length; an 8d nail is longer than a 4d nail (though *not* twice as long).

Screws are pointed-tip, threaded fasteners installed with a screwdriver. The type of screwdriver used depends on the screw head: straight (slotted), Phillips, Torx, etc. Slotted and Phillips are by far the most common screw heads. Screws are stronger than nails and easier to remove.

Bolts are threaded fasteners that typically use a threaded nut. Replace bolts with ones of the same head style, length, and thread (circular ridge). Bolts are stronger than screws.

Adhesives secure the surfaces of two materials together. Some work better than others with wood, plastic, metal, ceramic, fabric, carpet, or other materials. Some adhesives are more water resistant than others. Some adhesives work better on some types of plastics and not others. Read directions on various adhesive packages to determine what will work best for a specific application.

Shopping in a Hardware Store

Homeowners can find household parts, services, fixtures, materials, tools, and fasteners at retail locations called *hardware stores*. They range from hardware chain stores in small communities to mega-home-centers featuring enough materials to build a small community. Fortunately, most are designed to help the shopper find components relatively easily, especially homeowners who know about the basic systems within a home: structural, electrical, plumbing, heating and cooling, and security.

Most hardware stores are laid out in major departments viewable from the store's entryway. Signs are posted, typically high, to identify the departments. Within each department will be additional signs for specific components: Electrical—Lighting—Fixtures, for example. Or Tools—Plumbing—Wrenches.

Many larger stores have specialist clerks within departments who can answer specific questions or direct homeowners to needed parts and materials. Clerks in better hardware stores have worked in the construction and remodeling industries, so they know many of the answers. The difficulty is in phrasing the question in this new language of homeownership. The solution is to phrase the primary question before going to the hardware store:

■ What do I need to replace a single light switch?
■ Where can I find a replacement filter for my Hazagaga gas furnace model 12-20?
■ Where are ceiling patch kits, and how do I pick the right one for a 3-in (7.5-cm) hole?
■ How do I select the best paint for a kitchen?

EXPERT TIP: If you've never visited a large hardware store, do so and plan at least an hour of walking around to acquaint yourself with what is available and where it is located. In addition, you will discover how proactive the clerks are at offering assistance.

Once you have learned the systems within a typical house, specified how occupants are installed, identified the major parts, materials, and tools, and determined how best to find replacements, you're ready to begin maintaining your home.

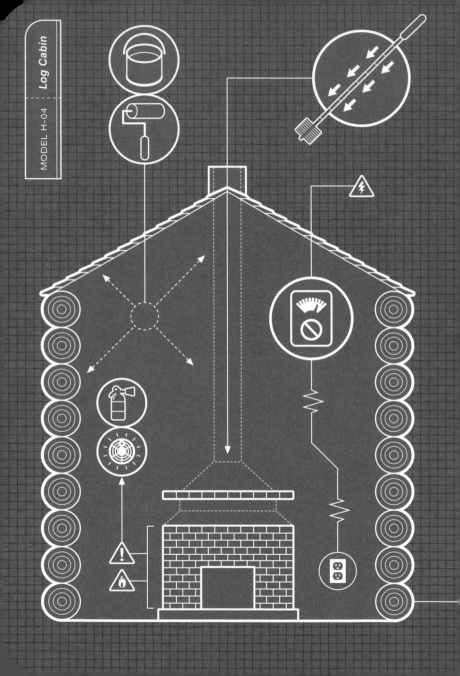

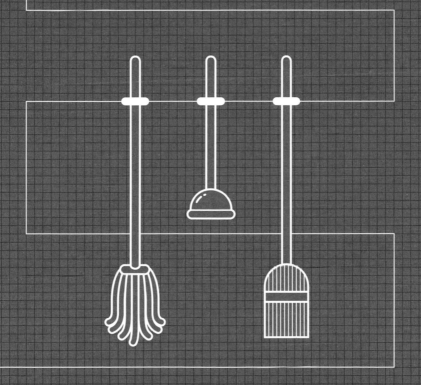

Chapter 4

Interior
Maintenance

Maintaining Home Interiors

The interior of a home includes all components within the living space: structural, electrical, plumbing, heating and cooling, and safety apparatus. Combined, these components enhance livability and convenience for the installed occupants.

Maintenance is the act of preserving what is. All home components are subject to wear and damage. Maintenance periodically renews the functionality of components by replacing worn or damaged components. Maintenance procedures are relatively simple and can be accomplished by any homeowner by following step-by-step instructions (see following pages in this chapter).

The job of interior home maintenance is best performed on an ongoing basis in anticipation of problems that may become home emergencies (see Chapter 6). Homeowners can perform basic maintenance tasks during the season prior to the component's primary usage, if applicable. For example, cooling system maintenance can be performed in the spring of the year and heating system maintenance in the fall of the year. Interior components that are year-round can be performed by priority, beginning with those that are most necessary.

Homeowners should perform a pre- or postacquisition inspection of all housing components (see pages 54–57). From this inspection, the homeowner can identify potential problems and future emergencies that can be proactively resolved with maintenance. In some living groups, this list is called the *job jar* or *honey-do list*.

Many homeowners find success in home maintenance by establishing a process for completing maintenance tasks. For example, a homeowner may perform these tasks on a Saturday morning, Wednesday evening, or other available period. Once the weekly task is completed, the homeowner will decide what maintenance function will be performed the following week and make a list of required components. Having the proper tools and materials on hand can dramatically reduce the time required to complete the task.

In some cases, the homeowner may choose to call for professional assistance to perform the maintenance task. For example, homeowners who don't have or prefer not to use long ladders may instead hire a chimney sweep or gutter cleaning service for these exterior maintenance tasks. An annual inspection by a licensed furnace service may be a good investment, and the homeowner can watch and learn how to perform the service in the future.

Following are interior maintenance projects and procedures that can be performed by most homeowners or adult occupants. Refer to Chapter 3 for additional information on tools and materials.

⚠️ *CAUTION: None of the following procedures are gender-specific. Attempting to make them so may void relationships.*

Structural Maintenance

Cleaning

The most common home maintenance task is cleaning. To maintain a neat and clean home with minimal effort:

[1] Put things away. Establishing logical storage locations for all household items reduces clutter. A child's floor, for example, is *not* a logical storage location for clothing.

[**2**] Set up a recycling point (usually in a utility room or a garage) where unused items are placed for recycling (weekly) or donation (monthly).

[**3**] Keep all cleaning products and tools together, and establish a routine for effective home cleaning. A plastic bucket with all primary cleaning products and tools can be taken from room to room as needed or as scheduled. A spray bottle of household cleaner and one of white vinegar with paper or cloth towels will suffice for most home cleaning tasks. Depending on toxicity, specialized cleaners (drain, tile, oven, wall, floor, carpet, furniture) can be grouped separately and secured from children.

EXPERT TIP: *Assign cleaning responsibilities to specific occupants with a motivating positive–negative reward system. "If the trash is emptied daily, bedtime is extended by 30 minutes," for example. Periodically review all cleaning tasks and the associated rewards to ensure that they are sufficiently motivating and not managerial tribulations.*

[**4**] Stop problems before they expand. Spilled water, juice, food, cosmetics, blood, and other fluids can quickly stain surfaces. Immediately use the cleaning bucket's cleaners and towels to minimize damage.

Maintaining Carpets

Fabric carpets and rugs require ongoing maintenance to keep them clean and in good condition longer. To maintain carpeting:

[**1**] Vacuum carpeting regularly to extend its life. Grit and debris combined with foot traffic can wear down fabric, especially in high-traffic areas near doorways and in hallways. For best results, make sure that the bag

is not full, the vacuum hose is not plugged, and the vacuum beater-head belt is not slipping.

[2] As needed, use carpet spot remover to ensure that stains do not deeply penetrate the carpet fabric. Pet urine stains, especially, can damage the fabric, backing, and padding below the carpet if not treated before they dry. Blot away excess liquid, then apply an oxygen cleaner following label directions.

EXPERT TIP: The primary advantage to professional cleaning is the power of the chemicals used and of the equipment that removes the dirt and chemicals during cleaning. Small low-powered home carpet cleaning machines cannot do as good a job as professional truck-mounted machines and should be used for interim maintenance cleanings only. Also, consider dry carpet cleaning machines and products, as they do not leave the carpet wet.

[3] Clean the carpet (or have it professionally cleaned) every six months or as needed. Low-traffic carpets and rooms can go a year or more without cleaning while high-traffic areas may need cleaning every three months. If possible, determine the carpet fabric type and cleaning requirements; some types require more or less cleaning than others. After five or more years, all carpets require more cleaning than when new.

Maintaining Door Locks

Doors are simple in design and require little maintenance except for their most complex components: locks. A lock is a mechanical fastener that secures a movable door to its stationary frame. Within the lock, the relationship of pins as determined by an inserted key allows or disallows the rotation of a cylinder. That rotation transfers to the movement of a

**bolt into an adjacent latch. When all works smoothly, the turn of a key
and knob immediately opens a door. Periodic maintenance and adjustment ensures that all works smoothly:**

[**1**] Twice a year, carefully spray lock lubricant (available at hardware
stores) into all household locks. Clean the lubricant from adjacent surfaces.
Also clean and straighten all keys so they easily insert into the locks.
Replace worn or damaged keys so they do not break off in a lock.

⚠️ *EXPERT TIP: Have household keys copied by a locksmith rather than
at a hardware store. Though the cost will be slightly higher, the results typically will be more accurate. Hiring a locksmith to remove a broken, poorly
copied key from a lock can be expensive.*

[**2**] Inspect each lock, latch, and doorknob every three to six months. Use
a screwdriver to tighten and realign loose components before further damage can occur.

[**3**] When inspecting locks, also check and tighten door hinges and
weatherstripping for a secure fit.

Painting the Interior

**Maintaining the interior of a home's structure begins with the cosmetic
and functional task of painting. Fortunately, painting is a relatively
simple maintenance project that can be performed by any homeowner.
The components include interior paint of the appropriate color(s), paint
brushes, paint rollers, and secondary equipment, such as a paint tray
and a drop cloth. To paint a home interior:**

[**1**] As needed, fill surface holes and repair damage (see page 99).

[**2**] Prepare the surface by washing it with a sponge and mild detergent. Remove any loose paint. If the surface is stained, cover with at least one coat of primer paint.

[**3**] Prepare the area with masking tape and a drop cloth to ensure that surrounding surfaces will not be painted. Remove any electrical outlet or switch covers. Cover or move nearby furniture and pets.

[**4**] Select the appropriate type of paint (ask a clerk in the paint section of a hardware or paint store) and application materials. Latex paint is preferred for most home applications. Enamel paint is preferred for kitchens and bathrooms, where moisture may be a problem. The finish—flat, semi-gloss, gloss—is a personal choice, though semi-gloss is the most popular.

[**5**] Using brushes, apply paint to the surface edges that a roller cannot easily cover, called *cutting in*.

[**6**] Apply paint with a roller to all flat surfaces easily covered with a roller. Paint in 3-ft (.9-m) square sections from the surface edges toward the center.

[**7**] Continue painting other room surfaces as needed.

[**8**] Allow the paint to dry (see paint-can instructions) before deciding whether to apply a second coat.

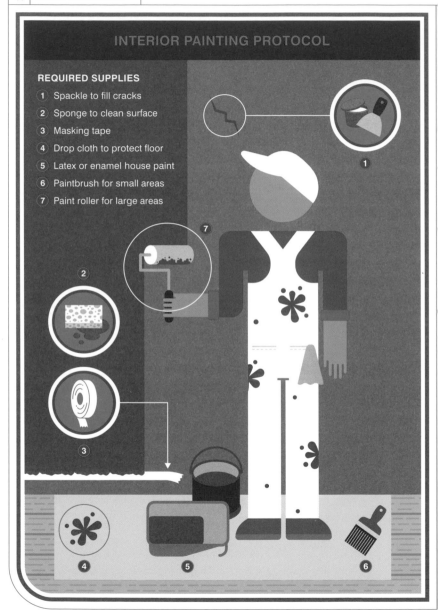

INTERIOR PAINTING PROTOCOL

REQUIRED SUPPLIES

1. Spackle to fill cracks
2. Sponge to clean surface
3. Masking tape
4. Drop cloth to protect floor
5. Latex or enamel house paint
6. Paintbrush for small areas
7. Paint roller for large areas

[9] If paint and equipment will be reused within 24 hours, drain leftover paint into the can and cover it. Wrap all rollers and brushes in cellophane or aluminum foil so they don't dry out. If the painting job is done, thoroughly clean all equipment following paint-can instructions.

See pages 170–178 for more comprehensive instructions on painting and decorating home interiors.

Filling Surface Holes

Walls and ceilings constructed of wallboard or lath and plaster (see pages 71–72) may require maintenance prior to interior painting. Fortunately, the process is relatively easy and there are numerous products available at hardware stores to make the job easier.

[1] Identify all imperfections on the surface before proceeding. Apply a small piece of masking tape on or near the imperfection for easier identification and remove when done.

[2] Use a putty knife or pointed object to remove any loose drywall. As needed, carefully hammer protruding wallboard nails to below the wall surface. If necessary, use joint compound to reattach loose wallboard tape that covers the seams between wallboard sheets.

[3] For smaller holes and dents, apply spackling following manufacturer's instructions (on the container). Drying time typically is 30 minutes.

[4] For larger damage, apply wallboard patch following manufacturer's instructions. Two coats may be required and the drying time may be longer.

[5] For holes larger than a large coin, use a wallboard patch kit that includes patch and fabric. Note that patch kits for ceilings use a sturdier fabric that will not sag when the patch is applied.

Electrical Maintenance

Inspecting Receptacles and Switches

Electrical receptacles, also known as *outlets*, and switches can become brittle with age and wires can come loose from their terminals, creating a hazard. To inspect receptacles and switches once a year for condition:

[1] Use a screwdriver to remove the receptacle or switch cover.

[2] Visually inspect the receptacle or switch, wires, and terminals without touching any of them.

EXPERT TIP: Once you are comfortable using a multimeter, you can test a live receptacle or switch to determine if electricity is flowing to the plugs. Refer to instructions for the multimeter and the receptacle or switch for directions (see page 101).

[3] If the receptacle or switch is brittle or the wires are loose, turn off the circuit at the main service panel before continuing. To verify that the circuit is off, turn the switch on and off or plug a lamp into the receptacle and turn it to the ON position. Alternatively, use a multimeter to make sure the circuit does not have electricity.

[**4**] To remove the receptacle or switch, first loosen the screws at the top and bottom that hold the unit into the electrical box. Then carefully pull the unit from the box with the electrical wires attached.

[**5**] To replace the receptacle or switch, first make sure the new unit is an exact replacement. Then remove the wire from one terminal and attach it to the corresponding terminal on the new unit before proceeding to the other wires. Once done, install the new unit in the box and reinstall the cover.

Inspecting Cords for Damage

Electrical cords deliver electricity from receptacles to portable appliances and fixtures. Because cords are flexible, they can be damaged and become an electrical or fire hazard. To inspect electrical cords every six months for damage:

[**1**] Unplug the electrical device or appliance for safety.

[**2**] Visually inspect the cord for cuts or other damage to the insulation that surrounds the wires. If minor, wrap electrical tape around the damage. If major, replace the cord (see step 4 below).

[**3**] Set a multimeter to read resistance (R) and touch the instrument probes to the two cord prongs. Turn device switches or controls to the ON position to close the circuit (though it is unplugged and no electricity is flowing). If the multimeter reading is 1 (infinite), the circuit is open and you have a bad circuit; otherwise, the circuit is closed, which is the desired reading.

ELECTRICAL RECEPTACLES AND SWITCHES

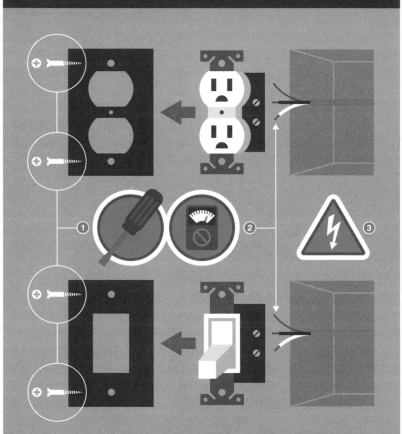

REMOVING AN ELECTRICAL RECEPTACLE OR SWITCH FOR MAINTENANCE

1. Use a screwdriver to remove the receptacle or switch cover.
2. Use a multimeter to test for electrical flow before handling any wires.
3. Turn off the electricity using the service panel if maintenance is required.

[4] If the circuit is open, the cause of a bad circuit could be the cord or the device. Manually move the cord around to see if the multimeter reading changes; it should not. If the reading changes, the cord may be damaged; replace the cord.

[5] To replace a cord, disassemble the device as needed to access the non-plug end of the cord. Make sure the replacement cord is of the same plug type and wire gauge as printed on the cord or on the tag attached to a new cord. Install the new cord and use a multimeter to test before using.

⚠ *EXPERT TIP: Many electrical cords have knots tied at the interior end to keep them from being pulled loose from their connection. Make sure you duplicate the length and connection of any cord you replace.*

Checking All Circuit Breakers or Fuses

Circuit breakers or fuses are safety devices in each electrical circuit within a home, typically installed within the electrical service panel. Homeowners should be aware of the location, function, and status of all circuit breakers or fuses within the home. To check the condition of all circuit breakers or fuses every three months:

[1] Find the home's electrical service panel. Most are located in an attached garage, near a front porch, or in a basement. In multiple-family dwellings, all electrical service panels may be located together in a common area.

⚠ *CAUTION: Turning off the wrong electrical service panel or a breaker that is being used by another household member—or another household— may cause personal static problems.*

[**2**] Visually inspect all circuit breakers or fuses within the electrical serv-ice panel. Breakers are black ON/OFF switches with the amperage indicated on the switch tip (15, 20, 30). Fuses are cartridge or screw-in devices with amperage indicated on the body. Most fuses have a viewable metal strip that indicates whether the fuse is burned or not.

EXPERT TIP: *Once removed, fuses can be tested using a multimeter set to resistance (R). Infinite resistance (1) means that electricity (from the multimeter's internal battery) cannot pass through the fuse and it is open, requiring replacement.*

[**3**] If the breaker is OFF, reset it by turning it back ON. If the fuse is burned, carefully replace it with one of the exact size, shape, type, and amperage. If the breaker again trips or the new fuse blows, do not use the circuit again until it is checked by a professional electrician.

EXPERT TIP: *In an emergency, you may need to find the correct breaker or fuse immediately to stop electrical flow in a circuit. In advance of any emer-gency, write the function of each circuit on a label near the breaker or fuse. You can determine the function with an assistant by turning off individual breakers or fuses to learn their function. For outlets, plug a lamp in to verify the circuit.*

Testing GFCI outlets

Ground-fault circuit-interrupters (GFCIs) are special electrical outlets required for installations near water sources, such as in kitchens and bathrooms. Water can easily become a path for electricity, as can a home occupant. GFCIs sense any nonstandard electrical path and immediately shut off (open) the circuit. To test GFCI outlets monthly:

[1] Identify a GFCI outlet. It includes two buttons, one black (sometimes blue or yellow) and one red.

[2] To verify whether the GFCI outlet is working, plug in a lamp or small appliance and turn it on. Alternatively, use a multimeter to test voltage (v) between the two plugs.

[3] To reset a GFCI outlet, first press the black button to turn off the circuit, then press the red button to turn it on. If it trips again, the outlet should be replaced (see pages 100–101). If a new GFCI outlet trips, a professional electrician should be called.

Plumbing Maintenance

Treating Slow Drains

Household drains must pass a wide variety of materials to the DWV system, some of it inappropriate to the system or more than it can handle. Accumulated grease, hair, and other materials can build up along the walls of drainpipes and slow or stop flow. To treat slow drains or periodically maintain them so they don't become clogged:

[1] Once a week, carefully turn on the hot water full force for 60 seconds to allow it to dissolve and push buildup within the drain and trap.

[2] Once every three months, carefully use a lye-based drain cleaner to flush all household drains following instructions on the package. For safety, wear rubber gloves and protective goggles to keep chemicals from eyes and hands.

⚠ **CAUTION:** *Harsh chemicals can be damaging to installed occupants and to the environment. To minimize their usage, use less caustic chemicals more frequently. Hardware stores offer numerous clog-cleaning products.*

[**3**] As needed, use a plunger, moving it up and down over the drain to develop suction that can break up debris. Immediately flush with hot water.

⚠ **CAUTION:** *Do not use a plunger immediately after using a drain cleaner or the suction will lift and spray the caustic cleaner. Allow water to run through the drain for at least one minute.*

For emergency procedures on drains, see pages 156–159.

Checking Pipes and Fixtures for Leaks

In the course of human events, some water must puddle. Unfortunately, standing water can damage other household components, so it is important that householders proactively maintain pipes and fixtures by periodically inspecting them. To check pipes and fixtures for leaks:

[**1**] Once a month, visually inspect the fresh water and drain components below each sink within the home. Look for moisture or evidence of water damage since the last inspection. Clean up any water and identify its source.

⚠ **EXPERT TIP:** *In bathrooms, condensation from showers or baths can collect on metal and ceramic fixtures, imitating a leak. To test, wipe away the moisture with a dry cloth and determine whether it quickly reappears. The best solution to condensation is proper ventilation through vent fans or an open window during showers or baths.*

[2] Touch each fresh water pipe connection below the sink and fixture with a finger. If the connection has a slow leak, droplets of water will form on the finger. Tighten the connection by hand or with a wrench as needed.

[3] As needed, run water through the sink drain and grasp each connection with a hand. If the connection has a slow leak, water will collect on the hand. Carefully tighten the connection by hand or with a wrench.

Draining Sludge from Water Heater

Water heaters are low-maintenance components that typically last ten or more years with little care. Periodic maintenance can double the life of a water heater. The most important task is to drain sludge and debris from the bottom of the water heater every six months:

[1] Turn off the hot water heater power, fuel, and water sources.

[2] Identify the draincock, similar to an outdoor faucet, located on the side of the tank near the bottom.

[3] Attach a garden hose to the draincock and stretch the hose out so it will drain to the exterior of the home or into a basement drain below the level of the tank.

[4] Carefully open the draincock to allow water to flow through the hose. As most sediment will be at the bottom of the tank, draining the entire tank is not necessary.

⚠💡 **EXPERT TIP:** *Excessive sediment, typically minerals from the water and rust from the tank lining, may indicate internal damage to the tank, requiring replacement.*

[5] Allow the tank to refill completely before turning the power to the heater back on.

Testing Water Heater Relief Valve

Excess heat and pressure can build up in a water heater, causing hot water to seek an outlet. For safety, hot water heaters have a built-in

WATER HEATER MAINTENANCE
1 Turn off water and power source.
2 Attach garden hose to draincock.
3 Open draincock with hose outside.

relief valve that is activated when contents exceed a specific pressure or temperature. This can occur if the thermostat that regulates the water temperature fails. To test the water heater relief valve every three months:

[1] Identify the location of the relief valve on the hot water heater. Typically it is located at or near the top of the hot water heater and includes an overflow pipe that points downward along the side of the tank to direct water away from the tank.

⚠ *CAUTION: Be especially careful when working around hot water heaters; water spray can burn skin or eyes. Wear safety glasses and protective gloves. If in doubt, turn off the water heater and allow it to cool down for at least four hours before testing the relief valve and turning it back on.*

[2] Place a bucket or other container below the tip of the overflow pipe to catch released hot water.

[3] Carefully lift up on the handle atop the relief valve to discharge water from the tank through the overflow pipe and to the bucket. Allow water to flow for about two seconds before closing the valve.

[4] If the relief valve fails the test, remove the attached tag and take it to a hardware or plumbing store to purchase an exact replacement. Alternatively, call a professional plumber for replacement.

Heating and Cooling Maintenance

Inspecting Systems

Heating and cooling systems are vital components to modern homes, especially in regions of extreme climates. There are numerous types of heating and cooling systems in homes, with the primary differences being the fuel source and the distribution method (see pages 80–82). Maintaining a home's heating and cooling systems begins with knowing what system is installed and where it is located. To visually inspect heating and cooling systems:

[**1**] Identify the home's fuel source(s). Depending on local availability and relative costs, homes within a region or built within a specific era tend to use the same fuel sources: electricity, gas, or oil. Some homes use one source for primary heating and another for supplementary heat. Air conditioning is fueled by electricity.

[**2**] Identify the type of heat production equipment. Many homes rely on a centralized heat producer, called a *furnace*, to heat air. Other homes use stand-alone heat producers, either fixed or portable, such as electric baseboard or wall heaters. Cooling and humidifying systems can be stand-alone or centralized equipment as well.

[**3**] Identify the type of distribution system. Some homes use forced-air distribution systems that allocate heated or cooled air to specific rooms through ducts and adjustable registers. Other homes use free-standing

motorized fans to push or pull treated air through the home. Still others use heated water or steam to heat metal registers that, in turn, warm the air. A few are designed to promote the natural movement of warmer or cooler air within the structure.

[4] Physically locate the home's heating and cooling components. Identify the location of the primary and secondary fuel source(s), the warm- and cool-air production equipment, and the distribution system components. This may require searching in a crawl space, basement, or attic to locate all components.

[5] Inspect each component for condition, evident damage, and the location of filters or other replaceable parts. Record model and serial number information in a notebook for easier access.

Cleaning Ductwork

Homes with forced-air distribution systems include ducts, aluminum or flexible pipes that distribute treated air to the home and return air to the heating or cooling unit for processing. For efficiency, it is important that these ducts be sealed from air leakage and that all obstructions are removed. To clean ductwork:

[1] Turn off the heating system and make sure that ducts are cool before beginning.

[2] Trace the ducts from the furnace through the home, typically ending at heat registers on or near the floor.

[**3**] Use a vacuum cleaner with a long handle to clean the ducts of any collected dust or debris. Access is through the furnace (turned off) or through heat registers in each room. Alternatively, purchase a tool designed specifically for cleaning ducts, available at hardware stores.

[**4**] If access is available, visually inspect the ducts looking for potential air leaks and apply duct tape (available at hardware stores) to seal seams and cracks in the ducts.

Cleaning or Replacing Filters

Home heating and cooling systems process hundreds of cubic feet of air each day, air that is laden with hair, pollen, and dust, microscopic critters that are potentially hazardous to health. Most closed air comfort systems include one or more filters to trap the larger of these elements. Some may include electronic filtration systems to collect more particles. Even stand-alone heating and cooling systems often have some form of filtration systems. To clean or replace filters:

[**1**] Identify the location and type of the system filter(s). Refer to the manufacturer's manual as needed.

[**2**] Remove the filter(s). Most are located on or near the furnace or cooling unit and often are identified on a label mounted to the unit.

[**3**] Clean or replace the filter. Some filters are replaceable with identical units available at hardware stores. Part numbers are on the filter, or they can be replaced with one of the same size. Other filters are cleanable with water. Use a garden hose to spray off the filter and allow it to fully dry before reinstalling.

[4] If the heating or cooling unit has a returning air duct, look for a filter at the primary return port or register. It may be a cleanable or a replaceable filter.

Checking Fans, Belts, and Motors

Most home heating and cooling systems have movable parts designed to force the flow of air to and from the comfort equipment. This equipment uses motors and belts to drive fans. Because they are moving, they are susceptible to wear and damage. Homeowners can minimize repair bills by periodically checking fans, belts, and motors in this equipment.

[1] For safety, turn off the furnace or cooling equipment at the electrical service box.

[2] Open the cover housing the equipment and identify the motor and, if accessible, the fan.

[3] Use a small vacuum cleaner or a cloth to carefully remove dust and debris from the motor, fan, and pulleys that connect the two.

[4] If there is a fan belt from the motor to other components, carefully inspect it for wear or damage.

[5] If the fan belt requires replacement, use a wrench to loosen the motor mount or pulley and release the fan belt. Write down the unit model number and take the old fan belt when purchasing a replacement at a hardware store. Reinstall and adjust the fan belt following the unit manufacturer's instructions.

Cleaning a Chimney

Wood fireplaces and some other types of heating sources have chimneys that allow smoke and gases to exit the structure vertically. Some of these by-products, including creosote, can build up on the chimney walls, creating a fire hazard. The primary solution is to burn hotter fires with fuels that have the least creosote. The secondary solution is to clean out the chimney once a year or as suggested by experience.

[1] Remove all movable fireplace components and tools, including the log rack.

[2] Cover the fireplace opening with plastic sheeting and fully seal it with duct tape to keep dust and debris from entering the room.

EXPERT TIP: *Wear safety goggles to keep floating dust from your eyes and a surgical mask to filter air to your mouth.*

[3] From the roof, insert a chimney brush (available at hardware stores) into the opening, using it to remove debris from the walls of the chimney. Start at the top of the chimney and work down to the fire box. Remove the brush.

[4] Wait at least one hour for the dust to settle before carefully untaping the fireplace cover.

[5] Use a shop vacuum to remove all dust and debris from the fireplace box and smoke shelf inside the chimney.

[6] Replace all fireplace components.

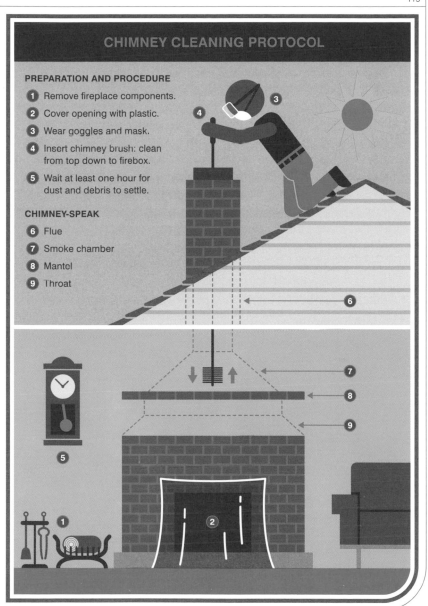

CHIMNEY CLEANING PROTOCOL

PREPARATION AND PROCEDURE

1. Remove fireplace components.
2. Cover opening with plastic.
3. Wear goggles and mask.
4. Insert chimney brush: clean from top down to firebox.
5. Wait at least one hour for dust and debris to settle.

CHIMNEY-SPEAK

6. Flue
7. Smoke chamber
8. Mantel
9. Throat

Cleaning Humidifiers and Dehumidifiers

Many climates require that water seasonally be added or removed from the household air for comfort. Humidifiers add water and dehumidifiers remove it. Humidifiers and dehumidifiers can be stand-alone units or attached to a forced-air distribution system. In either case, basic maintenance can enhance the comfort and health of a home. To clean humidifiers and dehumidifiers monthly:

[1] Identify the location of the equipment. Unless stand-alone, check on or near the furnace or cooler. Built-in humidifiers typically have a fresh water line attached to them, and dehumidifiers have a stale water line leading from them to a drain.

[2] Identify replaceable components. Drum humidifiers will have an absorption pad wrapped around a rotating drum. Dehumidifiers will have a dispersion pad at the exit side of the unit.

[3] Turn off the power and water to the unit.

[4] Remove and clean or replace these pads. At the same time, remove any trays or other detachable components and clean them with detergent. Apply bacteria-killing spray to all surfaces.

[5] Reinstall all components and write the date of the cleaning on a convenient surface for future reference.

Cleaning Radiators

Some home heating systems indirectly heat air through radiators. Hot water and steam systems produce hot water within a fueled boiler, and then distribute it to registers within far-flung rooms. These systems are most popular in larger homes and apartments, where rooms are remote, because water has less heat loss over distance than air. To inspect and clean radiators once a year:

[1] As much as possible, visually inspect all pipes between the boiler and each radiator. Some pipes will be in walls and floors, but may have false covers that allow inspection. If a leak or damage is identified, call a qualified plumber with heating system credentials.

EXPERT TIP: It's a good idea to know exactly where the main shutoff for a hot water or steam heating system is located as well as the shutoffs for each register.

[2] Make sure that the heater is off and cool before cleaning the radiator. Use a clean cloth with a small amount of soapy water or household cleaner to wipe down all surfaces. As needed, rinse away any residue.

[3] Visually inspect the radiator for signs of damage, rust, leaks, or other potential problems. If necessary, call a qualified plumber for repairs.

CAUTION: Because hot water and steam heating systems combine water pressure and high temperatures, they can be dangerous to work on. Don't attempt repairs without competent advice or hired professionals.

Bleeding Air from Hot Water Heating Systems

If a hot water heating system is not delivering heat to all rooms evenly or is producing a loud banging noise, air may be trapped within the system. Individual radiators can be bled to remove the air:

[1] Visually identify the bleed valve on the radiator. The owner's manual, if available, will indicate its location and offer specific instructions. Some bleed valves require a special tool supplied with the radiator when new.

[2] Set a bucket under the bleed valve.

[3] Open the bleed valve with a screwdriver or special tool.

[4] When water, instead of air, exits the valve, close the valve.

Safety Maintenance

Safety is the key to the longevity of a residence and its installed occupants. Modern and retrofitted homes have safety equipment—fire extinguishers, smoke detectors, etc.—that are on duty 24/7 but need periodic maintenance. Once every three months, carry out these homeowner responsibilities to make homes and occupants safer.

Checking Fire Extinguishers

There are three classes of fire extinguishers: A (for wood and plastics), B (for gas and oils), and C (for electrical). Costs are sufficiently low that homes can have A-B-C combination extinguishers throughout the home.

The most popular locations are the kitchen and a central hallway near bedrooms. To check and maintain fire extinguishers every three months:

[1] Visually inspect the charge status dial near the top of the extinguisher. If it indicates anything other than FULL, replace it with a new one. Alternatively, large professional extinguishers located in garages or larger kitchens can be refilled by fire extinguisher services (check the local telephone book).

⚠ **EXPERT TIP:** *Household fire extinguishers have a gauge that indicates whether the unit is FULL and, if not, printed instructions indicating what to do about it (recharge, discard).*

[2] Clean and visually inspect the units for condition, making sure the safety pin is firmly installed and the mounting bracket is resolutely attached to the wall.

[3] Reread the instructions for use and make sure that all adult occupants know how and when the unit should be operated. Also review the location of all fire extinguishers with occupants.

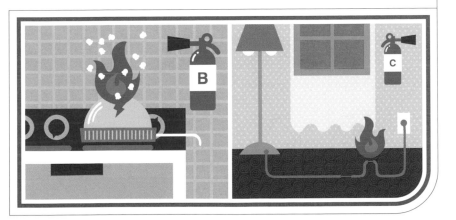

Testing Smoke Detectors

Once a month, smoke, gas, radon, and/or carbon monoxide detectors in the home should be tested:

[1] Identify the location of all hazard detectors within the home.

[2] Find and press the test button on the detector surface. If the detector does not respond with a shrill signal and/or flashing light, open the unit. Most detectors have a cover that is turned or unclipped for removal.

[3] If the unit has a battery, replace it with an identical battery and retest the unit. If the unit still does not function, replace the unit.

[4] If the unit does not have a battery, it is wired into the home electrical system; check the electrical service panel to verify that all circuit breakers are ON. Reset any that are OFF and retest the unit. If the unit still does not function, turn off the circuit and replace the unit.

Practicing Emergency Drills

The safety of installed occupants within a home relies on emergency planning. What will occupants do in case of a fire or other emergency? Planning and practice are required. Once every three months, practice planned emergency drills:

■ In case of fire, all occupants must immediately use the closest exit to the home's exterior and meet at a predetermined location safely away from the structure.

- In case of tornado, all occupants must immediately move to a predetermined location within the house that is below ground level, typically a basement or storm cellar.
- In case of an earthquake, all occupants must immediately move to predetermined locations within or outside of the house that are identified as safest from earthquake damage.

Replenishing the Survival Pantry

For safety, home occupants should plan and restock a survival pantry and room within the home that includes equipment and sustenance for the family unit. The planned duration depends on potential hazards identified by the unit. Families living in low-hazard rural areas may only require food and water for a two-day electrical outage, while urban families in areas of potential storm damage may require supplies and alternative energy sources for seven days or more.

[1] Based on local risks and conditions, plan a survival location and pantry within the home. Post a written inventory and update as needed. Stock it with at least three gallons (11 l) of water per person and a three-day supply of canned goods that can be eaten without any preparation. Include a manual can opener. Store a battery-powered radio, flashlights, extra batteries, a simple tool kit, and a first-aid kit.

[2] Once a month during hazardous seasons or quarterly otherwise, check and replenish food, water, and equipment as needed.

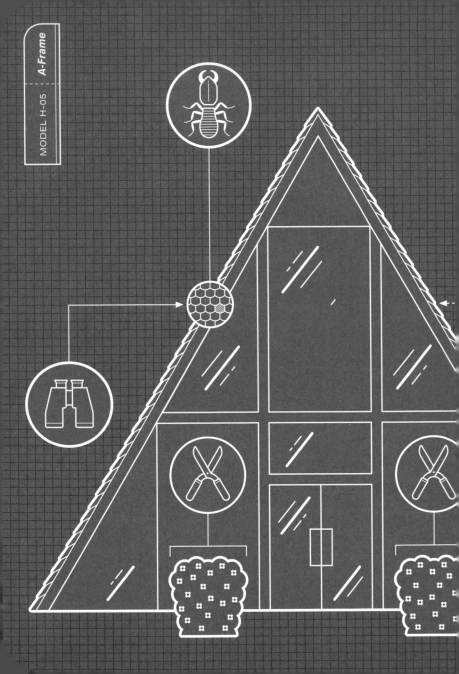

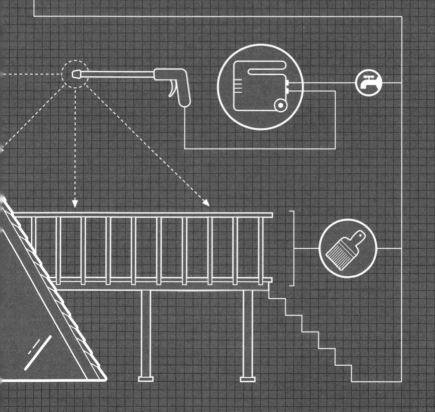

[Chapter 5]

Exterior
Maintenance

Maintaining Home Exteriors

The exterior of a home includes all components outside of the main living space: roofing, siding, doors, windows, decks, patios, walks, drives, yards, outdoor structures, and garages. These components are designed to augment and enhance the functionality of the home and the enjoyment of installed occupants.

Like the interior, a home's exterior requires periodic maintenance to renew its functionality. Exterior maintenance may require more effort than interior maintenance, but it can be satisfying work that extends the life and the livability of the home.

More than interior maintenance, working outside is seasonal, especially in extreme climates. However, many homeowners are motivated by the opportunity to be outdoors and do not mind exterior maintenance jobs in good weather. They find it more satisfying than wrong-season emergency repair work.

If the homeowner has developed a pre- or postacquisition inspection checklist (see pages 54–57), the primary exterior maintenance tasks are evident. As the appropriate season arrives, the homeowner and other occupants can plan the job, select proper tools and materials, and tackle the following tasks.

In some cases, professional assistance may be preferred or advisable. Climbing on the roof to apply a cleaner, for example, is not a task for all homeowners. In such cases, knowing how the maintenance task should be approached is valuable in selecting a qualified contractor or laborer.

Following are exterior maintenance projects and procedures that can be performed by most homeowners or adult occupants. Refer to Chapter 3 for additional information on tools and materials.

Roofing

Checking the Roof for Damage

A roof is the outside top covering of a home or other structure. Home roofs come in a wide variety of sizes, shapes, colors, and materials. Because they are exposed to the elements through many seasons and conditions, roofs can sustain damage that requires maintenance or repair. To inspect roofs for condition twice a year:

[1] From the ground, visually inspect each section of the roof for loose or damaged shingles. Binoculars are useful for this task. If required, use a ladder to inspect shingles more closely and repair or replace as needed. Asphalt shingles, the most common, are installed in sheets of three, called a *three-tab*, and nailed in place below the lip of the shingles above it using short roofing nails. Seams are staggered. Other roofing materials are installed as individual units or as rolls.

⚠ *CAUTION: Accessing a roof requires a ladder. For safety, make sure the ladder selected is sufficiently long that you don't use the top three rungs. Also, tip the ladder at least one-fourth of its length. For example, a 12-ft (3.6-m) ladder should be tipped at least 3 ft (.9-m) from the perpendicular. Make sure that your shoes are dry and the soles are corrugated for best grip when climbing the rungs.*

[2] Visually inspect all roofing for debris, moss, vegetation, or other materials that may lift roofing and allow water to enter the sheathing. If required, use a ladder and a long-handled grass rake to remove leaves or other debris. Use roof treatment chemicals (available at hardware stores) for killing moss or other live vegetation, making sure the chemicals don't damage nearby plants.

Checking the Attic for Water Stains

If the surface or protective barrier on a roof has been damaged, water can seep into the attic and into the home. To check the attic for water and other damage:

[1] Find the access to the home's attic. Most homes have a small lift-out panel or pull-down ladder located in a hallway or bedroom. Others will have an access door from an interior room into an adjoining attic.

[2] Carefully access the attic. Wear a hardhat or helmet to protect the head from nails protruding through the roof. Be careful to walk only on firm flooring or roof joists; a misstep can put a foot through the ceiling below.

[3] With a powerful flashlight or portable lighting device, inspect the underside of the roof sheathing for water stains and other potential problems. In addition, inspect the attic floor for damage caused by water dripping through the attic ceiling.

⚠️ **EXPERT TIP:** *Water runs downhill, so the point where water drips from a slanted attic ceiling may be lower than where it comes through the sheathing. Carefully inspect the bottom of the sheathing and all nearby rafters for other indicators of where the water is entering the attic.*

[4] If damage is identified, mark the location with a colored cloth or spray paint for later reference. Measure the distance from the spot to components that can be seen from outside the home (vent pipes, windows, dormers, etc.).

[5] Outside, identify the location of the leak using the measurements. Replace damaged shingles or remove vegetation (see page 140) as needed to correct the problem.

Cleaning Gutters

Gutters collect water that runs off the roof and distribute it through downspouts to the ground. Unfortunately, leaves and other vegetation also may fall to the roof surface and be swept into the gutters, clogging them. To clean roof gutters twice a year (depending on proximity to deciduous trees):

[1] Set a ladder on firm, level ground near the house. Climb up, and remove debris at the edge of the roof and in gutters beginning at the point farthest from the downspout.

EXPERT TIP: Some homeowners prefer to use waterproof gloves, a small garden trowel, and a bucket for this messy task.

[2] Use a garden hose with a pressure nozzle to remove dirt and debris from the gutter, starting at the point farthest from the downspout.

[3] Visually inspect the cleaned gutter for excess rust, holes, or other potential problems. Depending on the gutter material (aluminum, vinyl, wood) there are hardware-store products for repairing damage.

[4] Consider installing leaf traps over gutter surfaces to minimize debris.

Siding

Cleaning Siding

Siding is the home's skin. It can be made of wood, aluminum, vinyl, masonry (brick, stone), or one of many other materials. Because it is designed to withstand the elements year-round, it is durable and requires little maintenance. To clean home siding annually:

[1] Identify the home's siding type. Select cleaning products that match the siding's requirements. In many cases, a pressure washing with plain water is sufficient. If not, follow the cleaning product's directions for best results.

[2] Prepare the home for a pressure washing by making sure that the surface is repaired of any cracks or damage that can be exacerbated by the cleaning. Also cover any delicate plants near the home with contractor's plastic (light, clear, plastic rolled sheets available at hardware stores).

[3] Rent a pressure washer unit from a rental store, paint store, or larger hardware and home center store. Follow the instructions on the machine or ask the rental clerk to review them with you.

⚠ **EXPERT TIP:** *Wear safety goggles, a plastic cap, and old clothes when pressure washing a house, especially when using chemicals in the washer.*

[4] Test the washer on an inconspicuous location to determine how close to the house the pressure wand can be before paint or the siding material is damaged.

SIDING MAINTENANCE

CLEANING PREPARATION

1. Repair any exterior cracks or damage.
2. Wear the appropriate safety equipment.
3. Cover delicate plants with plastic.
4. Purchase or rent a pressure washer.
5. Test washer on inconspicuous area first.

[5] Use the pressure washer to clean the siding, beginning at the top of each side and working downward. If possible, start on the south side of the house before the sun heats the siding and the worker(s).

[6] Once complete, use a garden hose to wash down plants, driveways, and other areas of siding debris or chemicals.

Inspecting for Pests and Damage

Depending on the home's location, pests and weather damage can be a big problem for homeowners. At least twice a year, inspect the home's exterior for any damage and plan to fix it or get it fixed before further damage occurs:

[1] Ask a knowledgeable clerk at a local hardware store or home center what the local house pests are and how to identify them. In some areas, the pests are termites, wood beetles, or small bugs that typically leave a telltale trail or debris. In other locations, pests are unseen until the damage is already done.

[2] Visually inspect all components of the home's exterior, including the foundation, siding, eaves, window and doorframes, porches, decks, and other parts. Look for obvious damage and the possible cause.

[3] If pest or other damage is identified, either contact a professional or select products and materials to stop the cause and repair the damage. For the opportunity to bid on a project, pest control and repair contractors will assist in identifying the cause of specific damage.

Painting Siding

Wood and some other siding materials require periodic painting, typically once every eight to 12 years, or when the colors bore occupants, whichever occurs first. To paint siding:

[1] As needed, inspect the siding for damage and repair (see opposite page).

[2] Clean the siding to prepare it for paint adhesion (see page 128).

[3] Prepare the areas with masking tape and contractor's plastic to ensure that dripped paint will not land on other surfaces.

[4] Purchase primer, paint, and equipment, and get application advice from a knowledgeable paint or hardware store clerk.

[5] If the paint is worn from the siding surface or if the new color is significantly different from the old paint, plan to apply one or more coats of primer paint before applying the new color.

EXPERT TIP: Stain products are the least opaque, semitransparent stains are more opaque, and paints are fully opaque. Stains cannot be applied over paints without first removing all paint, a difficult task. A clerk in a paint store or paint department in a hardware or home improvement center can offer valuable expert advice in choosing paint or stain and the appropriate tools for applying the chosen product.

[6] Apply paint using larger brushes or rollers, depending on the type of siding. Spray painting can be problematic for inexperienced painters due to overspray. Start high on walls and work down to remove any drips.

[7] As needed, apply a second coat or any trim coats once the first coat has fully dried. Application and cleanup instructions are on the paint can.

Doors and Windows

Replacing Damaged or Worn Weather Stripping

Because doors and windows are designed to open and close, the seals between these barriers and their frames are not sufficiently tight to keep out all weather and keep in the home's conditioned air. Weather stripping fills the gaps. However, with use, weather stripping can be worn or damaged and need replacement. To maintain weather stripping once or twice a year:

[1] Open and close each exterior door or window in the home to identify the type and location of weather stripping. Most types are pressure weather stripping of soft material attached to the door or window; the weather stripping compresses against the doorframe when the door is closed.

[2] Inspect the condition of each weather stripping part. If the weather stripping is damaged, measure it, remove a sample, and take it to a hardware store for an exact replacement.

[3] Install the new weather stripping using nails or screws by referring to the old weather stripping.

Recaulking Windows, Doors, and Siding

Joints around nonmovable exterior components such as windows, doors, and siding can be weatherproofed with silicon caulk, a soft material that quickly hardens but remains pliable to fill gaps and reduce air and water leaks. Caulk is available in small or large tubes depending on the amount needed. Larger tubes require a caulking gun, a pressure device that forces caulk out the tip by squeezing a lever. To recaulk annually:

[1] Visually inspect the seam between siding and doors and windows for condition.

[2] Select the type and color of caulking appropriate to the task. Ask a hardware clerk for recommendations based on the application. Usage instructions are printed on the caulk tube.

[3] Remove any loose or dry caulking and replace with a new bead of caulking. Overlap as needed for a complete seal to ensure that water does not enter through the gaps into the home. Pests, too, can enter through gaps or damaged caulking.

Checking Window Seals

Newer windows have more than one thickness or pane of glass. The area between panes may be airtight or filled with an insulating gas. If the seal around the panes leaks or is damaged, air and moisture can enter or gas can escape, making the insulation less effective. Replacing the seal is a job for a professional window glass service or contractor. However, the homeowner can perform a quick inspection once or twice a year:

[**1**] Visually inspect each window, looking for condensation (moisture) between the panes.

[**2**] On a very cold day (if locally available), go outside and touch each windowpane. If one of the panes is warmer than others, it may be allowing heat to exit the home through a poorly sealed pane. Inspect for warped or damaged neoprene seals around the edge of the pane.

[**3**] As needed, call a glass service or window contractor for a second opinion before buying a replacement pane or window. Most window units will require removal and replacement rather than allow on-site repair.

Decks

Pressure Washing Decks

Wood decks are exposed to rain, snow (optional), wind, and other elements throughout the year. Depending on the level of exposure, decks should be cleaned with a pressure washer, a gas-powered engine that forces water through a nozzle at a velocity higher than a garden hose with a pressure tip. To pressure wash a deck every year or two (depending on age and condition):

[**1**] Identify the deck material. The surface can be pressure washed with water or, if there is moss or other substances on it, a cleaner can be used following the product instructions.

[**2**] Prepare a deck for a pressure washing by making sure that all protruding nails or bolts are tightened. Cover any plants with plastic sheets.

[**3**] Rent a pressure washer unit from a rental store or a larger hardware and home center store. Follow the instructions on the machine or ask the rental clerk.

⚠ **EXPERT TIP:** *Wear safety goggles, a plastic cap, and old clothes when pressure washing a house, especially when using chemicals in the washer.*

[**4**] Use the pressure washer to clean any vertical surfaces, such as deck railings.

[**5**] Wash the deck surface in the direction of the boards, moving away from the house.

[**6**] Once complete, use a garden hose to wash down plants and other nearby components of debris or chemicals.

Recoating Decks

Most decks require periodic recoating to minimize weather damage. The type of coating depends on weather exposure and the decking material. Common wooden decks in four-season climates require recoating every two to four years. Newer wood or plastic decking only requires pressure washing. To recoat a wood deck:

[**1**] Identify the deck material (redwood, cedar, fir, pine, composite) and select a recoating product manufactured for application on horizontal surfaces. A hardware store or home center clerk can assist in selection and suggest application.

DECK COMPONENTS

1. Ledger
2. Joist hanger
3. Joist
4. Bridging
5. Girder
6. Post
7. Post hardware
8. Pier
9. Decking
10. Rail
11. Baluster
12. Tread
13. Stair stringer
14. Barbecue grill
15. Grill master

MAINTENANCE

A. Pressure wash every 1–2 years

B. Recoat deck every 2–4 years

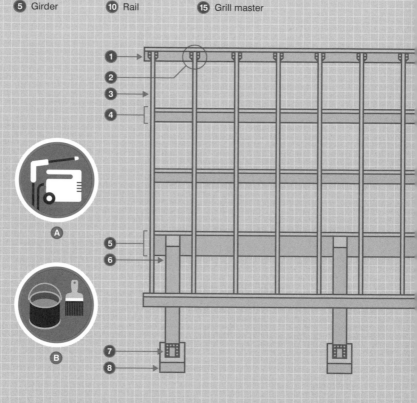

EXTERIOR DECK: A deck is a relatively inexpensive addition to the home

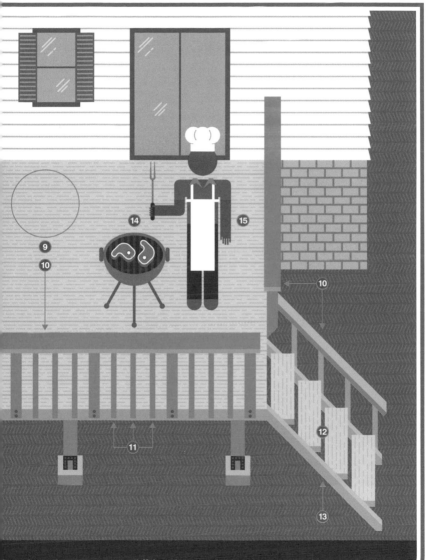

hat gives the occupants additional space for outdoor entertainment of guests.

⚲ **EXPERT TIP:** *Make sure you have good weather for the recoating job: not too hot or cold with little or no wind that will distribute dust and debris on the wet surface.*

[**2**] Follow the coating manufacturer's instructions. Typically this requires pressure washing the surface (see page 134) followed by application with a special tool designed for horizontal application.

⚲ **EXPERT TIP:** *Plan the job so you don't paint yourself into a corner.*

[**3**] Allow the surface to fully dry before using it or moving deck furniture back on it.

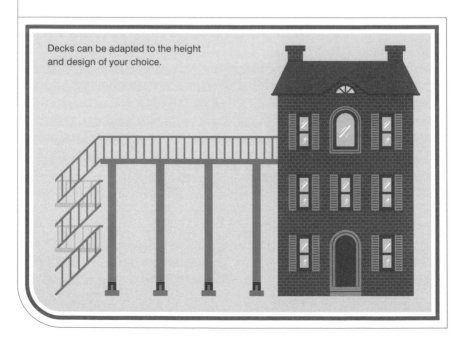

Decks can be adapted to the height and design of your choice.

Patios, Walks, and Drives

Patios, walks, and driveways are horizontal surfaces of concrete, asphalt, rock, or other nonorganic products. They, too, are subject to wear and damage and require periodic maintenance.

Pressure Washing Patios, Walks, and Drives

To pressure wash patios, walks, and drives annually:

[1] Identify the surface material. Concrete typically is light in color and smooth; asphalt is black and rough. Some walkways are made of concrete with inset stones. The surface can be pressure washed with water or, if there is moss or other substances on it, a cleaner can be used following the product instructions.

[2] Prepare a surface for pressure washing by removing all debris and covering any delicate plants near the home with contractor's plastic sheets.

[3] Rent a pressure washer unit from a rental store or home center store. Follow the instructions on the machine or ask the rental clerk for directions.

[4] Wash the surface away from the house or plants and toward any drains.

[5] Once the task is complete, use a garden hose to wash down plants and other nearby components of debris or chemicals.

Patching Surfaces

[1] Identify the surface material: concrete (gray) or asphalt (black).

[2] Select appropriate patching material available at a hardware store or home center.

[3] Follow the product instructions. Typically, clean any loose pieces from the area to be patched. If it is deep, a hole may require placing sand or small rocks at the bottom as a foundation for the patch. Install the patching material and spread or tamp the surface for a smooth plane.

[4] Allow the patch product to dry as instructed. Protect the surface from moisture, excessive heat or sunlight, and use until fully dried or cured.

Yard Maintenance

Living trees and shrubs around a house will enlarge, sometimes endangering the structure. Pests can use plants as a stairway to the house. Tree branches can grow close to a fireplace chimney or heat system vent and become a fire hazard leading to loss of the dwelling. Yard maintenance includes cutting problematic plants away from the structure. To annually trim plants away from the house:

[1] Identify potential problems. Visually inspect each plant near the house, including trees that may fall on the structure.

[2] Select and remove any branches or other plant components that can damage the home in a windstorm or serve as access for termites, ants, or other pests.

[**3**] Remove any loose debris from around the house that can become a nest or a fire hazard.

EXPERT TIP: *Many communities have recycling services that will pick up yard waste. If not, local businesses advertised in newspaper classified ads typically offer yard cleanup services and runs to the local dump.*

Outdoor Storage Structures

Maintaining Siding

Outdoor sheds and other structures furnish protected storage space for yard and lawn equipment, playthings, and yard chemicals. These structures require periodic maintenance, including painting.

[1] As needed, inspect the siding for damage and repair (see page 130).

[2] Clean the siding to prepare it for paint adhesion (see page 128).

[3] Prepare the areas with masking tape and contractor's plastic to ensure that dripped paint will not land on other surfaces.

[4] Purchase primer, paint, and equipment, and get application advice from a knowledgeable paint or hardware store clerk. Prepare and paint outdoor structures to complement the house colors and design.

[5] Apply paint using larger brushes or rollers, depending on the type of siding. Start high on walls and work down to remove any drips.

[6] As needed, apply a second coat or any trim coats once the first coat has fully dried. Application and cleanup instructions are on the paint can.

Maintaining Doors and Hinges

Outdoor storage structures are simple in design with few moving parts. Those moving parts, however, require periodic maintenance. To maintain doors and hinges annually:

[1] Visually inspect the structure's doors and hinges, looking for loose or broken components.

[2] Tighten all loose fasteners. If screws spin when turned, use larger screws or fill the screw hole with wood. Lubricate hinges as needed.

EXPERT TIP: Loose screw holes can be filled with toothpicks pushed into the hole then broken off at the surface.

[3] If necessary, remove broken or bent hinges or latches and take them to a hardware store to select replacements. Take the screws as well. Install new components and align them. Reinstalling hinges may require a helper to hold the door in place.

Garages

Cleaning Garage Floors

Garage floors collect automotive fluids and other stains that not only are unsightly, but can also damage the flooring material and require repairs. To clean and maintain garage floors every month or two:

EXPERT TIP: Buy a small container of garage floor cleanup, available at auto stores and some hardware stores. Whenever a grease spot is identified, spread the cleanup (similar to sand) on the spot and allow it to soak up the liquid and draw from the concrete before sweeping it up.

[1] Remove all vehicles and large items to visually inspect the floor for damage.

[**2**] Sweep or vacuum the floor surface. If necessary, patch the floor (see below).

[**3**] Apply a degreaser or shop cleaning product to any oil stains on the floor following the manufacturer's directions. Mineral spirits is a good cleaner for oils.

⚠ *CAUTION: Don't store shop rags that have oil or gas on them, as they may self-combust if stored long-term. Instead, use heavy-duty paper towels for cleanups and immediately seal them in a plastic bag and throw them away.*

[**4**] As needed, periodically use a household cleaner to keep the floor clean for use and storage.

Patching Concrete

Cracks are common in concrete garage floors, especially in areas of seismic activity or with a concrete slab that is poorly installed. Larger holes require repair similar to that for patios, walks, and drives (see page 140). To patch smaller cracks in concrete garage floors:

[**1**] Clean dirt and debris from the crack, sweeping or vacuuming out anything loose.

[**2**] Apply concrete repair patch (available at hardware stores) following directions on the package. Alternatively, smaller surface cracks can be repaired with concrete caulk to keep water from entering the crack and causing further damage.

Maintaining Garage Doors

Entry doors are the primary moving components of a garage, and so are subject to wear and damage. Periodic maintenance is a good investment in minimizing costly repairs. To maintain garage doors every six months:

[1] Inspect each component of the garage door, including rails and rollers, for damage and wear.

[2] Lubricate the roller bearings and rollers with lightweight oil.

EXPERT TIP: If the power goes out, you can open an automatic garage door by pulling on the release rope above the door and manually lifting the door from the inside.

[3] Tighten any loose bolts, screws, or other connectors to ensure that the mechanism tracks smoothly.

[4] Replace the battery in all garage door opener remotes.

[5] Check and replace light bulbs in the garage door opener.

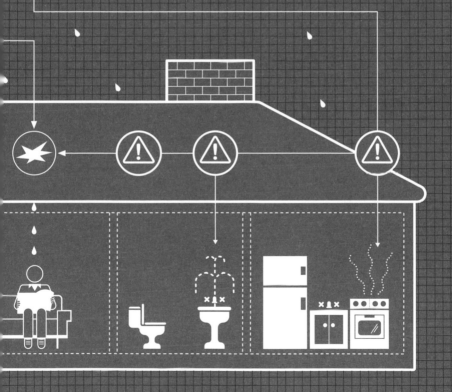

[Chapter 6]

Emergency Repairs

Avoiding Emergencies

Emergency repairs often occur because the homeowner (or a prior homeowner) is unaware of the need for and steps and benefits of ongoing maintenance (see Chapters 4 and 5).

To avoid emergency repairs, establish and follow a systematic interior and exterior maintenance schedule. It will save repair costs and time. It is less time consuming to perform periodic home maintenance than to make emergency repairs. A conscientious homeowner can defer a repairperson indefinitely.

Following are common emergency repairs that can be performed by most homeowners or adult occupants. Refer to pages 84–87 for additional information on tools and materials.

Structural Emergencies

Damaged Siding

Home siding can be damaged by wind, falling objects, or imprecise drivers, making the interior accessible to the elements. Fortunately, the homeowner can minimize damage by responding quickly to the emergency. To repair damaged siding:

[1] Visually inspect the damage to identify the cause and extent. If the damage is cosmetic, use additional time to plan the repair project. If it is structural and can quickly lead to other problems, take action as soon as it is safe to do so.

EXPERT TIP: Depending on the severity of the damage and the potential for ongoing harm, cover the area with contractor's plastic sheets as soon as possible.

[2] Identify the extent of the damage and the materials needed to repair it. A split to a single wood siding board can be repaired in place with construction glue and nails. Vinyl and aluminum siding can be patched using products available at hardware stores. Greater damage may require replacing one or more boards or siding sheets.

[3] As needed, install replacement components. Wood siding typically is overlapped and attached with nails, screws, or other fasteners. Vinyl siding is clipped into place using a zip tool (available at hardware stores). Aluminum siding is nailed or clipped into place depending on the design.

[4] Finish the job cosmetically by painting (see pages 131–132) the surface to match surrounding surfaces.

Rotten or Eaten Wood

Some siding emergencies develop over time as pests gain access to wood siding or structural parts. Various types of regional pests thrive on housing components. Periodic inspection and maintenance (see page 131) will minimize the need for repairs. However, deferred maintenance by prior homeowners can eventually necessitate structural or siding repairs:

[1] Identify the extent of the damage. Use the tip of a knife or screwdriver to probe exposed wood (siding, floor joists from under the house) and identify loose shards and dust-like debris. Rotted wood crumbles or breaks away easily.

[2] Identify the cause of the damage. Damage from surface pests is more easily recognized than damage from subterranean pests. Moisture and fungi typically damage wood from the outside in.

[**3**] Remove the cause of the damage. Apply chemicals to kill the pests (or hire a pest exterminator to do so). If moisture is the cause, find and remove the source, which often is standing water caused by a diverted exterior drain.

[**4**] Repair or replace damaged materials. If the damage is superficial, remove any destroyed material and seal the area with paint or a sealer (available at hardware stores). If the damage is structural, replace damaged components or hire a contractor to do so, depending on the extent and repercussions of the damage.

Leaky Roof

Once the cause and location of a leaky roof is identified (see page 125), the next task is to repair it.

⚠ **CAUTION:** *Working on a roof or ladder can be dangerous; always work safely. As necessary, wear a safety belt and rope firmly attached to a chimney or a stationary object on the opposite side of the house.*

[**1**] Stop the leak. If the leak is around a chimney or DWV pipe, the cause may be a loose metal or plastic flashing (seal). Inspect the flashing for damage and replace or reattach as needed, applying caulk around the edges. If the leak is around a shingle, reattach or replace the shingle and underlying roofing paper.

💡 **EXPERT TIP:** *Water runs downhill. As replacement shingles and flashing are repaired or replaced, remember that components must overlap with the higher piece partly covering the top of the next lower piece.*

[2] Repair the damage. Asphalt shingles can be repaired by applying a small amount of roofing cement (available at hardware stores) to fasten them to the surface or to patch a hole. If damage is more extensive, remove damaged shingles or flashing as needed to eliminate the cause of the damage. If roof sheathing or roofing paper is damaged beyond repair, carefully replace it with new material using a small pry bar and roofing hammer to remove nails and shingles.

Electrical Emergencies

Fixing Appliances

Major home appliances include washers, dryers, dishwashers, refrigerators, stoves, ovens, and microwaves. What they have in common is that they are mechanical and/or heating devices with control systems. Because of this commonality they are similarly repaired.

Portable appliances also are mechanical and/or heating devices powered by electricity. Small appliances include blenders, can openers, clocks, coffee makers, cookers, espresso makers, food mixers, hair dryers, heating pads, rice cookers, shavers, toasters, and vacuum cleaners. They, too, can be tested and repaired with a multimeter, common tools, and common sense. To repair an appliance:

[1] Check the breaker or fuse for the circuit at the electrical service panel. Reset or replace as needed.

[2] Check the appliance cord for damage. Unplug the cord and use a multimeter to test the cord (see pages 101–102).

[**3**] Check all controls for damage. As necessary, disassemble the appliance to access switches and other controls. Use a multimeter to test the controls for proper action. (Instructions for testing controls are included in some appliance owner's manuals and in multimeter instruction sheets.)

⚠ **EXPERT TIP:** *Some major appliances have a reset switch on the back, typically near the cord, that must be reactivated after it has been tripped. Also, many electronic appliances have troubleshooting codes that can be requested and read with information from the owner's manual.*

[**4**] Visually inspect components, looking for obvious damage, wear, or blockage.

[**5**] If necessary, call an appliance repair technician for further assistance or replacement parts. Describe the symptoms and actions taken.

[**6**] If the appliance cannot be economically repaired, recycle it. When purchasing a replacement, make sure the new unit is designed to minimize the problems that caused the initial appliance to fail.

Restoring Electrical Power

Modern living is dependent on consistently delivered electrical power. Breaks in service, surges, or brown-outs (reduced power) can damage electrical devices and frustrate a home's installed occupants. To restore electrical power and prevent damage to electrical components:

[**1**] Anticipate loss of electrical service. If electrical storms are predicted

(Fig. A), unplug all electronic devices (TVs, stereos, computers) that can be damaged by electrical surges or outages (Fig. B).

[2] If an electrical outage occurs without warning, turn off all electronic devices and unplug major appliances (Fig. B) so the return of power doesn't overwhelm circuits (some appliances draw more power on startup than during operation).

[3] If the outage seems isolated within the home, go to the electrical service box and inspect circuit breakers (Fig. C) and fuses for proper status (see page 103).

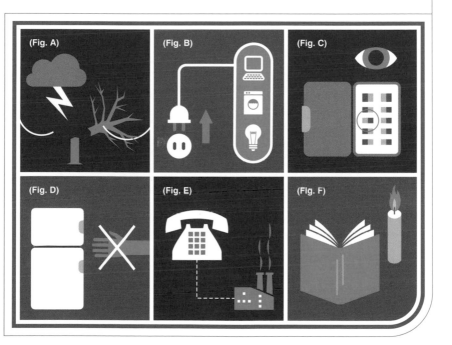

[4] If the outage may be more than two hours, do not open the refrigerator unless absolutely necessary (Fig. D); doing so will result in the loss of cooled air. Check the home's survival pantry (see page 121) for needed food and supplies.

⚠ **EXPERT TIP:** *If an outage lasts more than 30 minutes, call the electrical service supplier (Fig. E) to notify them of the outage or to get an estimate of when power may return. Telephone numbers are on electrical bills and in the front of most telephone books. Do not call 911 unless the outage causes a medical emergency.*

[5] Find a candle and read a good book (Fig. F).

Plumbing Emergencies

Leaky Faucet

The most common emergency repair in many homes is fixing a leaky kitchen or bathroom faucet. There are different types of faucets (see pages 78–80). If the faucet has only one lever for both hot and cold water, it is a cartridge or ball type. If the faucet has two handles that rise when the water is turned on, it is a compression valve faucet. If the handles lower when water is turned on, it is a reverse-compression valve.

To repair a cartridge or ball faucet:

[1] Turn off the water supply to the faucet.

[2] Use an Allen wrench to remove the faucet handle.

[**3**] Carefully unscrew the retainer nut by hand or with adjustable pliers and remove it from the faucet.

[**4**] Remove the cartridge or ball stem from the faucet body. Some cartridges are held in place with a retainer clip.

[**5**] If the cartridge, ball, or O-rings are damaged or worn, replace them. Replacement parts are available at hardware stores and typically include installation instructions.

[**6**] Reassemble the faucet, turn on the water supply, and test the faucet for leaks.

To repair a compression or reverse-compression faucet:

[**1**] Turn off the water supply to the faucet.

[**2**] Remove the trim cap on the faucet using a small screwdriver or utility knife.

[**3**] Remove the locknut and lift the spindle out of the faucet.

[**4**] As needed, remove and replace the O-ring, washer, and seat. Replacement parts are available at hardware stores and typically include installation instructions.

[**5**] Reassemble the faucet, turn on the water supply, and test the faucet for leaks.

Clogged Kitchen Drain

Kitchen drains are designed to efficiently remove soiled water from the sink and adjacent dishwasher. If the sink includes a garbage disposer, it also removes ground-up food waste. However, if the drain is asked to pass products more viscous than vegetable soup, it may store excess within the drain until capacity is reached and flow stops. To unclog a kitchen drain:

[**1**] Remove all dishes and the strainer from the sink. Use a container to remove excess food, water, or debris from the sink.

[**2**] Place a sink plunger (available at hardware stores) over the drain, force it down to compress it, and then lift it to develop suction in the drain line (Fig. A). If the dishwasher is attached to the sink's drain line, use duct tape or a rag to seal the air-gap tube located near the faucet.

[**3**] If the drain is still clogged, insert a plumbing auger (available at hardware stores) into the drain to clean it out (Fig. B). Drains with garbage disposers do not have direct access from the drain to the sink trap below.

[**4**] If the drain is not yet clear, place a plastic dishpan or bucket under the J-shaped sink trap pipe and carefully loosen the nuts that hold it in place (top and bottom). Thoroughly clean or replace the trap and clean out the connecting drainpipe before reassembly (Fig. C).

[**5**] If the kitchen drain still does not drain, the cause may be deeper into the drain line. Either use an auger to clear it or call a professional plumber (Fig. D).

UNCLOGGING A SINK

(Fig. A)
USING A PLUNGER

(Fig. B)
USING AN AUGER

(Fig. C)
CLEANING THE SINK TRAP PIPE

(Fig. D)
CALLING A PROFESSIONAL

EXPERT TIP: *Plastic dishwashing gloves are useful when unclogging a drain. They are thin enough to unencumber dexterity while protecting the hands from drain debris and chemicals.*

Clogged Bathroom Drain

Bathroom drains are simple in operation. Water flows through the drain, into a J-shaped trap, then through drainpipes within the wall to the sewer or septic system. Bathroom drain clogs typically are caused by accumulated hair on the sink stopper or within the trap. To unclog a bathroom drain:

[**1**] Remove the sink stopper. Some lift or screw out while others are attached to a stopper control that must be wiggled to release the stopper from the drain.

[**2**] Place a sink plunger (available at hardware stores) over the drain, force it down to compress it, and then lift it to develop suction in the drain line.

EXPERT TIP: *Though household drain cleaners may be used (carefully) for clearing clogged drains, they are more useful (and safer) for drain maintenance (see page 105). Using caustic chemicals in a drain, then disassembling the drain, can be hazardous to the health of maintenance personnel.*

[**3**] If the drain is still clogged, insert a plumbing auger (available at hardware stores) into the drain to clean it out.

[**4**] If the drain is not yet clear, place a plastic dishpan or bucket under the J-shaped sink trap and carefully loosen the nuts that hold it in place (top

and bottom). Thoroughly clean or replace the trap and clean out the connecting drainpipe before reassembly.

[5] If the bathroom drain still does not drain, the cause may be deeper into the drain line. Either use an auger to clear it or call a professional plumber.

Clogged Toilet

Few plumbing emergencies are as urgent as clearing a clogged toilet. The best way to avoid the problem is not to use the toilet for disposing of objects it is not designed to handle. To unclog a toilet drain:

[1] If the bowl is full, use a handled container to bail out half of the water. If the bowl is empty, add water until it is half full.

[2] Place a toilet (not a sink) plunger over the bowl drain and rapidly move it up and down. Once water drains from the bowl, repeat the process to ensure that it is clear.

EXPERT TIP: A sink plunger looks like a ball cut in half. A toilet plunger looks more like a misshapen ball with a large hole on the bottom. Each is designed for a specific type of fixture. In fact, using a toilet tool in a kitchen sink is a potential health hazard.

[3] If the plunger does not clear the blockage, insert a plumbing auger into the drain and push it until the blockage is reached. Rotate the auger to snag, move, or break up the blockage. If this operation is successful, follow up with the plunger to ensure that all blockage is removed.

[**4**] If the auger and plunger do not clear the blockage, call a plumber who has professional equipment and additional knowledge.

Broken Pipes

A broken water pipe can be a big emergency, especially if it's not found until additional damage is done to the home's structure or contents. To repair a broken water pipe:

[**1**] Turn off the water that feeds the broken pipe. If the damage is between a shutoff and a fixture, turn the shutoff to stop water flow. Otherwise, find and turn the main water shutoff to stop water flow to the house. If a closer shutoff is found later, it can be used and the main shutoff turned back on.

⚠️ *CAUTION: Standing water can easily conduct electricity. When working on a broken pipe, wear rubber-soled shoes and keep all electrical appliances and wiring away from the area.*

[**2**] Place a plastic pan or bucket under the leak to catch water and minimize damage to other household components. Clean up any standing water in the area.

[**3**] If the break is small, patch the damaged pipe. Measure the pipe diameter and the width of the break. Pipe patch products are available at hardware stores and can be used to cover and seal the break in the pipe.

[**4**] If the break is larger, repair the damaged pipe. Measure the pipe diameter and the width of the break(s). Depending on the pipe material (copper, cast iron, plastic), replace a section of the pipe using pipe material and con-

nection fittings. Hardware clerks can help in selecting the appropriate pipe and fittings and any special tools needed.

⚠ **EXPERT TIP:** *To determine whether your home has ongoing water leaks, first make sure that all faucets and water appliances (washer, dishwasher) are turned off and the water heater has not been recently used. Next, find the municipal water meter for the house, typically in a ground box near the street or front of the house. The meter dials should not be moving. If they are, there may be an undetected leak in the line from the meter to the house or within the house. It's time to look further or call a plumber.*

Leaky Basement

Unexpected water in a home basement can become an emergency if the problem is not resolved before damage spreads. Even an uninhabited crawl space under the house can become a hazard if standing water is allowed to damage the foundation or subfloor. To repair a leaky basement:

[**1**] Remove any carpet, rugs, or furnishings that could be damaged.

[**2**] Remove any standing water. If the water is deeper than 1 in (2.5 cm), rent a sump pump to remove the water as quickly as possible.

[**3**] Search for the source of the leak. If the source is a broken pipe, repair it (see opposite page). If the leak is caused by a faulty exterior drain or gutter downspout, clear any blockage or redirect the drain. If the leak is caused by a crack in a concrete foundation wall, prepare the area and apply a concrete patch material following directions on the container.

No Hot Water

The hot water system serving a home takes in fresh water from the municipal water service or from a private water well, heats it using gas or electricity, and keeps it at a set temperature until requested by an occupant who turns a hot water faucet or starts a load of laundry. If an occupant discovers that there is no hot water available, follow these steps:

[1] Check other hot water faucets to determine if the problem is in an individual fixture or the source, the water heater. If the problem is in the fixture, check for a broken pipe (see page 160).

[2] Carefully touch the water heater to determine if it is functioning. If it is a gas water heater, make sure it is getting fuel and that the pilot light is on. If it is an electric water heater, make sure its circuit breaker or fuse in the electrical service panel is operational.

⚠ *CAUTION: Water heaters store hot water under pressure, so be careful working around them. An inoperative thermostat and relief valve can allow internal heat and pressure within a water heater to rise to the point that it becomes explosive.*

[3] To relight a gas water heater, first turn off the controller and allow gas in the air to dissipate. Follow the directions on the controller for relighting the pilot, typically by holding down the pilot button and using a match to light the pilot through a nearby access port.

💡 *EXPERT TIP: If the home has a single water heater, it usually is located in the basement, in an attached garage, or near bathrooms and the kitchen, often in a small closet or behind a movable wall panel. Larger homes may have more than one water heater, smaller and located in individual bathrooms or the kitchen.*

Leaky Water Heater

A water heater that leaks water can increase water costs as well as damage nearby possessions. Because hot water is under pressure, leaks that develop can quickly expand. Periodic inspection of the home's water heater(s) (see pages 107–109) can minimize costly problems. To fix a leaky water heater:

[**1**] Identify the source of the leak. If it is at the junction of the tank and a pipe, tighten the fitting. If it is at a tank seam, replace the tank.

⚠ *EXPERT TIP: When working around a hot water heater, wear safety goggles and protective gloves.*

[**2**] To tighten a fitting, first turn off the fuel source and release tank pressure. Use a plumber's wrench to tighten each pipe fitting to and from the tank. Also tighten the draincock and the pressure relief valve fittings. If replacement is required, consider hiring a plumber.

[**3**] To replace a tank, first turn off the fuel source and release tank pressure. Once the tank is cool, drain it of all water. Turn off and disconnect the fuel source. Install the replacement tank following the manufacturer's instructions. Or consider hiring a plumber.

Heating and Cooling Emergencies

Fuel Leak

Heating systems require fuel to warm the air. Fuel leaks can be danger-ous to a home and its residents or at least expensive if undetected. Depending on the type of fuel used, consider installing a fuel leak detector (available at hardware stores) near the home's heating fur-nace. In case of a heating fuel leak, follow these instructions:

[**1**] If the smell is simply a pilot light that has gone out, turn off the furnace and allow any gas to dissipate before relighting. Lighting instructions are posted on or near heater controls.

[**2**] If the problem is a fuel leak, evacuate the house. If the leak is propane or other gas, leave doors and windows open to allow the fumes to dissipate.

[**3**] Turn the fuel source off outside the home. Oil and gas storage tanks have shutoffs.

[**4**] From a cell phone or neighbor's phone, call the fuel company and ask for assistance. If help is unavailable, call the fire department.

No Heat

Though not having heat may not be an emergency, it can be a major dis-comfort. If prolonged or if temperatures become extreme during the winter, it can become an emergency. If the home has no heat:

[**1**] Check the thermostat to make sure it is ON, in the correct mode (HEAT), and that the set point is appropriate. If necessary, turn the thermostat set point to a *higher* temperature. Most heating systems require two to five minutes to respond to setting changes.

[**2**] Check the fuel supply or, if the system is electric, the circuit breaker or fuse.

[**3**] As necessary, use a secondary heating system (fireplace, space heaters) as the heat source while troubleshooting the primary heating system.

[**4**] Be sure the door to the furnace is secure. Many furnace doors have an interlock switch that stops the furnace motor if the door is opened while in operation.

[**5**] Visually and aurally inspect the furnace for obvious problems, such as a loose drive belt or the repeated clicking of control relays. If a problem is found, turn off the furnace power and fuel sources and call a heating system technician.

No Cooling

Cooling system problems typically occur on days when they are least appreciated. If the home cooling system quits functioning:

[**1**] Check the thermostat to make sure it is ON, in the correct mode (COOL), and that the set point is appropriate. If necessary, turn the thermostat set point to a *lower* temperature. Most cooling systems require two to five minutes to respond to setting changes.

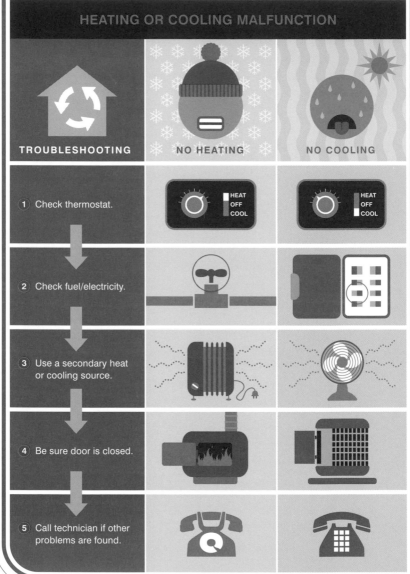

[**2**] Check the air conditioner's or cooler's circuit breaker or fuse.

[**3**] As necessary, use a secondary cooling system (stand-alone air conditioner, evaporative cooler, fans) as the cooling source while troubleshooting the primary cooling system.

[**4**] Be sure the door to the air conditioner is secure. Some unit doors have an interlock switch that stops the coolant pump or fan if the door is opened while in operation.

[**5**] Visually and aurally inspect the unit for obvious problems, such as a clogged filter, popped reset button, or unusual internal noises. If a problem is found, turn off the cooling unit's power and call a cooling system technician.

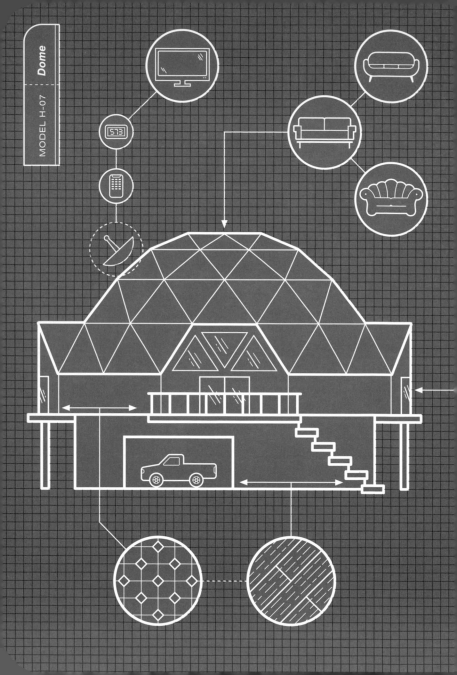

MODEL H-07

Dome

Chapter 7

Options

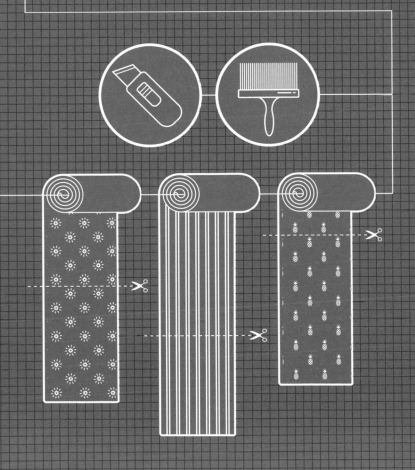

Decorating Basics

New homes typically are decorated in neutral colors, offering the first homeowner the option of adding hue and furnishings. Previously owned homes may include colors and components that don't fit the tastes of the new homeowner. In both cases, the solution is decorating.

To decorate is to ornament or beautify, subject to preferences. These predilections can be translated into colors and components by the homeowner(s), living group members, or by professional decorators depending on the tastes, skills, and budget of the subject occupants.

The primary methods of decorating homes are by painting, installing other wall coverings, and installing flooring. In addition, occupants will decorate with furnishings, to taste.

Interior Painting

Chapter 4 provided instructions for interior maintenance including painting. Many homeowners also use paint as a decorating material. Doing so requires more planning and effort than simple paint maintenance. However, the steps are the same: prepare the surfaces, choose the paints, select the appropriate tools, gather additional materials, perform the painting process, and clean up the area and materials when done.

Preparing Surfaces

Interior surfaces that can be painted include walls, ceilings, and trim, including doors and windows. In each case, the surface must be prepared for application of the paint to optimize product adhesion and longevity. To prepare most surfaces for paint requires repairing and cleaning.

To repair surfaces before painting:

[**1**] Identify all surface imperfections on walls, ceilings, and trim within the selected room(s). Apply a small piece of masking tape on or near the imperfection for easier identification and removal when done.

[**2**] Use a putty knife or pointed object to remove any loose wall material. As needed, carefully hammer protruding wallboard nails to below the wall surface. If necessary, use joint compound to reattach loose wallboard tape that covers the seams between wallboard sheets.

[**3**] For smaller holes and dents, apply spackling following manufacturer's instructions (on the container). Drying time typically is 30 minutes.

[**4**] For larger damage, apply wallboard or plaster patch (depending on the type of wall) and patch following manufacturer's instructions. Two coats may be required and the drying time may be longer.

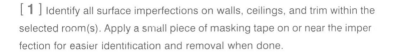 *EXPERT TIP: Wallboard patch kits that include fabric and patch material are available at hardware stores. Select the size and type (wall or ceiling) required to make the repair and follow manufacturer's instructions.*

To clean interior surfaces for painting:

EXPERT TIP: Select the type of cleaner appropriate to the surface: drywall, paint, wood, or masonry. Ask your hardware clerk for recommendations.

[**1**] Purchase a box of trisodium phosphate (TSP) from a hardware or paint store and follow mixing directions on the package. Typical mixing ratio

is $1/4$ to $1/2$ cup of TSP per gallon (50–100 ml of TSP per 3 liters) of water for medium- to heavy-duty cleaning projects. Alternatively, there are other less caustic (and less effective) surface cleaners available at hardware stores.

⚠ **CAUTION:** *Trisodium phosphate is a strong cleaner that can injure eyes and unprotected skin. Wear cleaning gloves and eye protection when using TSP. If skin comes in contact with TSP, immediately wash it with water. Do not use TSP on metals or plumbing fixtures. Once the surface is cleaned, TSP must be rinsed from any surface. TSP is not available in all areas.*

[**2**] Apply the cleaner to the surface following manufacturer's instructions. Typically, use a clean cloth or sponge that has been dipped in the cleaner and wrung out. Excessive moisture can damage unprotected drywall.

[**3**] Rinse the surface to remove any residual cleaner. Use a clean cloth or sponge dipped in clean water and wrung out.

[**4**] Allow the surface to dry thoroughly before applying primer or paint.

Choosing Paints

A wide variety of paints is available and most consumers find the selection process as daunting as the application process. However, professional assistance from hardware and paint store clerks can make both tasks easier.

Paint Types

Paints are a mixture of color (pigment) in a liquid vehicle: water-based latex paints or solvent-based alkyds. Paints with linseed oil, also known as oil-based paints, are alkyd paints. Latex paints are popular for most interior and exterior surfaces because they hold up well to use and are easy to clean. Alkyd paints are more durable and more waterproof.

Latex paints may include additional ingredients to make them last longer or clean more easily. A stain is a finish formulated with transparent or semi-transparent color to allow the painted surface to be visible; it is especially popular as an exterior wood finish. Acrylic is a synthetic resin that extends paint life. Epoxy is a synthetic petroleum resin that makes paint even more durable. Enamel paint has a smooth, hard finish for special applications, such as major appliances.

Primers are similar to paints except that they are intended to cover and seal the surface. Primers are used when the surface is damaged, stained, or of a color very different from the selected top-coat paint. Hardware and paint store clerks can assist in choosing an appropriate primer if needed for interior or exterior paints.

The best pigment or color of paint is subjective. However, decorating experts suggest that warmer colors be used in north-side interiors, pastels in south-side interiors, and lighter or cooler colors in interior rooms on the east or west side. Exterior home colors are selected to either blend in or contrast with surroundings, depending on the installed occupants' tastes.

EXPERT TIP: When selecting paint colors, narrow the search using color cards available at paint centers, then purchase and apply a sample of paint before the final color selection. All paints look slightly different from the color cards once applied, depending on the surface material, prior colors, room light, and other colors within the room. Once the paint is selected, make sure the clerk records the color name or formula on the top of the can in case more is needed later.

Selecting and Using Painting Tools

Primary painting tools include appliers (brushes, rollers, pads) and supporting equipment (paint trays, ladders). Electric and pneumatic paint sprayers are an option, but for all but the largest painting tasks the application time saving is lost to preparation and cleanup. Pressure pumps that deliver paint to special rollers or pads can reduce painting time, though they increase prep and cleanup time. The choice depends on the size of the job and the frequency of repainting.

Common paintbrushes include:

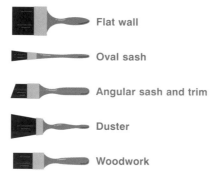

Flat wall

Oval sash

Angular sash and trim

Duster

Woodwork

Paintbrushes are available with natural bristles or synthetic bristles or are made of foam. Homeowners who plan larger painting jobs often invest in natural-bristle brushes, thoroughly cleaning them after each use for long life. Natural bristles are preferred for alkyd paints. Synthetic brushes are cost-effective for painting one or two rooms every few years and are preferred for latex paints. Disposable foam brushes are useful for smaller and touch-up painting jobs because cleaning is not required.

Paint rollers include a frame (sometimes called a "birdcage") with handle and a roller cover. As with brushes, better-quality roller covers are most efficient for bigger or higher-quality jobs. Select short-nap ($1/4$-in/.6-cm) roller covers for smooth surfaces, $1/2$-in (1.3-cm) nap for textured surfaces, and $3/4$-in (2-cm) nap for stucco, concrete block, and other rough surfaces. Standard rollers are 9 in (22.9 cm) wide, but narrower trim rollers are available for smaller areas.

Paint pads are useful for smaller jobs or for trim. Paint trays allow the roller or pad to absorb the paint and to remove excess.

EXPERT TIP: For easier cleanup, line a paint tray with aluminum foil that can be discarded when the job is done.

Selecting Other Painting Materials

There are numerous other tools and materials available to make painting easier and cleanup faster. The most popular are painter's tape and painter's (or contractor's) plastic. Painter's tape is similar to masking tape except with less adhesion to make it easier to remove. Standard widths are 1 in (2.5 cm) for masking windowpanes and other small areas, and 2 in (5.1 cm) for attaching painter's plastic to edges. Painter's plastic comes in 15 in (38.1 cm) folded rolls that can be spread to 9 ft (2.7 m) for covering exterior plants, interior furniture, and other items that don't require painting. The plastic can be cut as needed with household scissors and taped down with masking tape.

EXPERT TIP: Painter's plastic is cheaper and much easier to use than most cleanup products, so apply it generously to cover the work area as well as to protect nearby objects. However, if it is spread on the work floor, remember that the surface can be slippery.

The Painting Process

For most painting jobs, paint window and door trim before painting surrounding walls. Trim typically has more edges and curves that are difficult to paint evenly. Trim paint can overlap on to the surrounding wall and later be cut-in or covered over with the wall paint for smoother results.

To paint door and window trim:

[**1**] Paint horizontal surfaces before painting vertical ones.

[**2**] Apply paint to the central sections of doors and windows before applying it to outer edges.

[**3**] If painting to an edge, apply paint horizontally to near the edge, then paint vertically up to the edge for greater control and smoother results.

To paint rooms and large surfaces:

[**1**] Remove all switch covers, outlet covers, and lighting fixtures. If components cannot be removed, apply painter's masking tape around the object to protect it from paint application.

[**2**] Remove all small furnishings from the room. Large furniture may be moved to the center of the room and covered with painter's plastic.

[**3**] As needed, repair (see page 99) and clean (see page 170) the room's surfaces.

[4] As needed, apply a primer coat to patched areas.

⚠️ **EXPERT TIP:** *Paint ceilings before painting walls.*

[5] Using brushes or pads, apply paint to the surface edges that a roller cannot easily cover, called *cutting in*.

[6] Apply paint with a roller to all flat surfaces easily covered with a roller. Paint in 3-ft (.9-m) square sections from the surface edges toward the center.

[7] Continue painting other room surfaces as needed.

⚠️ **EXPERT TIP:** *To minimize accidents, always place the paint container at the approximate same location relative to the painter and move the container as needed. If the painter doesn't know where the can is, he or she may accidentally kick and spill it.*

[8] Allow the paint to dry (see paint can instructions) before deciding whether to apply a second coat or to use sponges and other decorative tools to install designs on the wall.

Cleaning Up

Efficient cleanup can make the painting job easier. The primary advantage to latex paints over alkyds is that they are water-based and easier to clean up with water. Alkyd paints require paint solvents to clean brushes, rollers, and other equipment. The advantage of disposable brushes is that there is no cleanup necessary, though they can be cleaned and reused.

⚠ **EXPERT TIP:** *If the painting job is not done and will be continued within 24 hours, paint brushes can be wrapped tightly in cellophane or aluminum foil without cleaning. If the job will continue within a few days, brushes can be wrapped and placed in the freezer.*

To clean up after a completed painting job:

[**1**] Wipe excess paint from the can lip and exterior, then replace the lid. To seal the can without splattering paint, place a newspaper over the lid before pounding the lid into place.

[**2**] Use old rags or shop towels to remove excess paint from brushes, rollers, pads, and equipment.

[**3**] Clean all brushes, rollers, pads, and equipment as needed with water (latex paints) or solvents (alkyd paints). Allow all components to thoroughly dry before storage.

[**4**] Dispose of all waste materials safely. Wrap unusable latex paint materials in plastic bags. Check with local waste management services on the method of disposing of solvents.

⚠ **EXPERT TIP:** *Allow empty latex paint cans to dry in the sun, then pull out the solidified layer of paint for disposal and recycle the can.*

Wall Coverings

There are numerous other wall covering products available besides paint. Paneling, once popular, is being replaced by wallpaper and other, more decorative materials. Wallpaper, the most popular wall covering, also is being installed on walls that were previously painted. (Modern wallpaper is made of paper, vinyl, and other products.)

The primary advantage to wallpaper is the colors, patterns, and textures available that are difficult to duplicate with paint and other wall products. Cost can be lower than other products as well, especially if the homeowner is willing to absorb the labor requirements.

EXPERT TIP: Visit a wall covering store or large home center for samples of the latest wallpapers. Besides paper and vinyl, coverings are available in foils, flocks, fabrics, and other products. Relief wallpapers give surfaces texture. Murals can offer scenic decoration to a room. Young occupants love room murals.

Preparing Surfaces

Successful wallpaper installation requires quality preparation. The covering needs a clean, smooth surface to which it can adhere. To prepare wall surfaces for wallpaper:

[1] Remove any existing wall covering products. Paneling is held in place by nails that can be pulled or adhesive that can be heated for removal. Old wallpaper may be removable by hand, using removal chemicals, or by steamers. To determine the best removal procedure, practice on a section in a closet or behind a door.

⚗️ **EXPERT TIP:** *Wallpaper steamers and other removal tools are available at larger rental centers. Ask the rental clerk for operating instructions.*

[**2**] Repair the wall surface (see page 99) as need to make the surface smooth.

[**3**] Clean the surface with TSP or other cleaner (see page 170) as needed. Rinse the wall and allow it to dry. Follow any preinstallation procedures included with the new wallpaper.

Installing Wallpaper

Various types of wallpaper are available, depending on the labor-saving features of the material. Unpasted wallpaper, prepasted wallpaper, and adhesive wallpaper products offer different degrees of convenience and cost. Unpasted wallpaper requires the homeowner to apply a special glue paste on the back side of the paper before installation. Prepasted wallpaper necessitates dipping the wallpaper in water to activate the glue paste. Adhesive wallpaper requires that a backing cover is removed before installation. Instructions for preparing unpasted, prepasted, and adhesive wallpaper typically come with the product.

To install prepasted wallpaper:

[**1**] Paint all window, door, and wall trim (see page 176) before installing wallpaper.

[**2**] Beginning in the least conspicuous corner of the room, mark and hang the first sheet with a $1/2$-in (1.3-cm) overlap on to the adjoining wall.

INSTALLING WALLPAPER

UNPASTED **PREPASTED** **ADHESIVE**

PASTY PASTE

1. Paint all trim first.
2. First sheet overlaps adjoining wall ½ in (1.3 cm).
3. Squeeze out air bubbles with brush or squeegee.
4. Trim top and bottom with scissors or utility knife.
5. Cut sheets at least 6 in (15 cm) longer than wall.
6. Overlap sheets by ½ in (1.3 cm).
7. Match pattern.

Make sure the sheet is perpendicular and the pattern is level. Use a wallpaper brush or squeegee to press out any air bubbles from behind the paper.

[**3**] Carefully trim the wallpaper at the top and bottom using scissors or a utility knife.

[**4**] Cut the next wallpaper sheet at least 6 in (15 cm) longer than the wall to allow for pattern matching.

[**5**] Install the next wallpaper sheet, overlapping by $^1/_2$ in (1.3 cm) and matching the patterns. Trim top and bottom.

[**6**] Continue around the room, carefully trimming around windows, doors, and other permanent wall components.

Flooring

Decorating a home also includes replacing flooring. Homeowners can select and install a wide variety of flooring products with simple or rentable tools. These products include carpeting, hardwood, hard tile, and vinyl-composition tile (VCT).

Installing Carpeting

Carpeting is the most popular flooring material. Although most homeowners prefer to hire carpet installers to do the work of installation, simple jobs can be completed without professional help. Carpeting is sold in rolls, typically 12 ft (3.6 m) wide, that are cut before delivery and seamed when installed. Padding is delivered in rolls and cut on-site to

fit. **Installation materials and tools include tack strips (for attaching the carpet edge to the subfloor edge), seamers and tape, and door threshold trim. To install carpeting:**

[**1**] Level the subfloor or any prior flooring surface, filling in rough spots or gaps.

[**2**] Install tack strips (sold at large home centers) around the room perimeter using a hammer and saw.

[**3**] Install the carpet padding up to the edge of the tack strips and tack it in place with a construction stapler.

[**4**] Roll out and cut the carpet to fit the room, joining pieces as necessary with hot-glue seam tape and a seaming tool (available at rental stores).

[**5**] Use a power stretcher and knee kicker (available at rental stores) to stretch the carpet and attach it to the perimeter tack strips.

[**6**] Carefully trim the carpet edges at the wall with a utility knife.

Installing Hardwood Flooring

Hardwood flooring has evolved over the past 20 years to become an easier-to-install product that fits more homes and decorating budgets. Old hardwood floors were $3/4$-in (1.9-cm) thick and required on-site sanding and finishing. New hardwood floors, $3/8$- to $3/4$-in (0.95- to 1.9-cm) thick, are prefinished and ready to edge-nail into place. The latest laminate flooring materials are thinner and interlock

without nails for easy installation. To install interlocking or edge-nailed hardwood flooring:

[**1**] Level the subfloor or any prior flooring surface, filling in rough spots or gaps.

[**2**] For floating floors, install foam backing on the subfloor. For wood strip flooring, install adhesive as recommended by the manufacturer.

[**3**] Install the first strip of flooring, following manufacturer's instructions, along the longest wall in the room, making sure the interlocking edge faces away from the wall. For edge-nailed flooring, use a flooring nail gun (available at rental stores) to install the first row.

[**4**] Continue installing flooring across the subfloor, interlocking or nailing as required by the type of flooring.

[**5**] Trim edge pieces as needed to fit near edge walls and the final wall.

[**6**] Install trim around wall edges and thresholds at any doorways as suggested by the flooring manufacturer.

EXPERT TIP: Installing flooring is the subject of many books. The instructions here are offered as guidelines for homeowners to determine whether their skills are appropriate to the task or whether a professional flooring contractor should be hired.

Installing Hard Tile

Ceramic and other hard tiles can be installed by ambitious homeowners; the task isn't difficult, just labor-intensive. To install hard tile flooring:

[1] Level the subfloor or any prior flooring surface, filling in rough spots or gaps.

[2] Mark the starting point and reference lines on the floor. The starting point is near the room's center, adjusted to minimize the number of tiles needing cutting at the room's edges. Set two reference lines perpendicular to one other, intersecting at the room's center. The reference lines form a cross at the starting point to guide the laying of tiles.

[3] Spread the tile adhesive using a grooved trowel following manufacturer's instructions. Typically, adhesive is spread over small areas to make installation easier.

[4] Lay the first tile at the starting point and between the two reference lines.

⚠ *EXPERT TIP: If grout will be installed between tiles, use tile grout spacers (available at hardware and flooring stores) in between tiles to allow space for grouting after tiles are installed.*

[5] Lay following tiles adjoining the first tile and touching one of the two reference lines.

[6] Continue installing tile flooring across the subfloor.

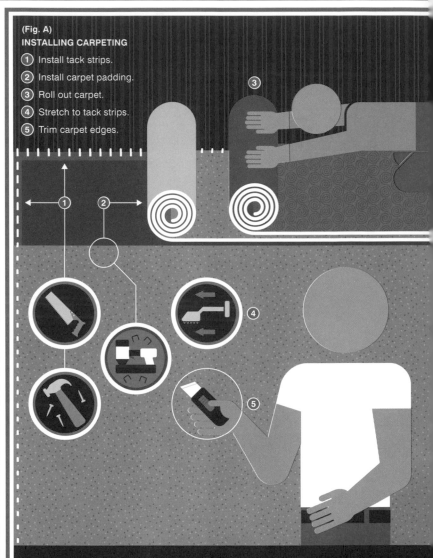

(Fig. A)
INSTALLING CARPETING

1. Install tack strips.
2. Install carpet padding.
3. Roll out carpet.
4. Stretch to tack strips.
5. Trim carpet edges.

INSTALLING FLOORING: Before installing any type of flooring, it is

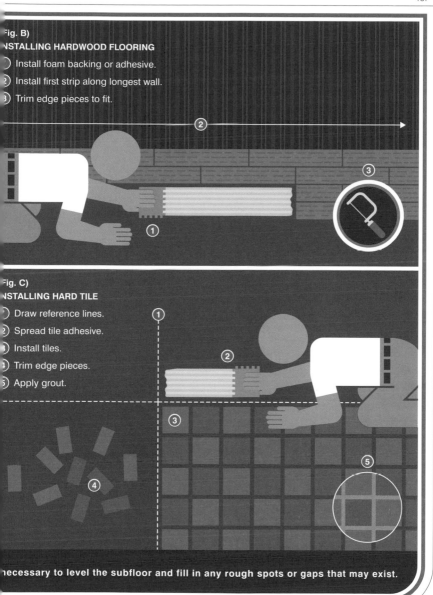

Fig. B)
INSTALLING HARDWOOD FLOORING

1. Install foam backing or adhesive.
2. Install first strip along longest wall.
3. Trim edge pieces to fit.

Fig. C)
INSTALLING HARD TILE

1. Draw reference lines.
2. Spread tile adhesive.
3. Install tiles.
4. Trim edge pieces.
5. Apply grout.

necessary to level the subfloor and fill in any rough spots or gaps that may exist.

[**7**] Trim edge pieces using a tile cutter (available at rental stores and some home centers) and install them.

[**8**] If grout is to be installed, remove spacers and follow grout manufacturer's instructions. Typically, the grout mix is forced into the space between tiles and the excess removed. Tile surfaces are washed and rinsed before use. Some grout products require a final sealing to keep water out. Ask the flooring clerk at your local hardware store for recommendations.

Installing VCT

Vinyl-composition tile (VCT) is also known as *vinyl flooring*, *resilient flooring*, and by the older name of *linoleum*, no longer in use. VCT is available in rolls or squares. Installation for both formats is approximately the same:

[**1**] Level the subfloor or any prior flooring surface, filling in rough spots or gaps.

[**2**] If installing square tile flooring: Mark the starting point and reference lines on the floor. The starting point is near the room's center, adjusted to minimize the number of tiles needing cutting at the room's edges. Set two reference lines perpendicular to one other, intersecting at the room's center. The reference lines form a cross at the starting point to guide the laying of tiles.

If installing roll flooring: Make an actual-size paper template of the room including any cutouts for plumbing fixtures. In a larger space, such as on a garage floor, use the template to cut the roll flooring to size.

[**3**] Spread the tile adhesive, following manufacturer's instructions. Typically, adhesive is spread over small areas to make installation easier.

Alternatively, some VCT is installed with staples at the room perimeter, and VCT tiles may have an adhesive exposed by removing a paper backing.

[4] Install trim to cover the flooring edges and install door thresholds as needed.

Getting Professional Help

The decorating procedures in this chapter are instructional. They serve as an overview of the process of painting, installing wall coverings, and installing flooring. Additional instructions from a manufacturer, retailer, or other books are needed for actual installations, depending on products and skill levels.

The alternate function of these instructions is to help homeowners decide whether the task is doable by an installed occupant or should be left to hired professionals. If professionals are hired, the instructions assist the homeowner in knowledgeably discussing the project.

A *contractor* is someone hired with a written contract to perform a specific job. A *general contractor* is a generalist who may do the job or hire a subcontractor to do the actual work. Contractors are licensed by the state, but not all home decorators require licensing. Handypersons who may do painting, wall covering, and flooring installations may or may not be state licensed. The advantage of licensing to the consumer is additional recourse if there is a problem, but state licensing doesn't guarantee quality workmanship.

Larger home improvements, called *remodeling*, are covered in the next chapter.

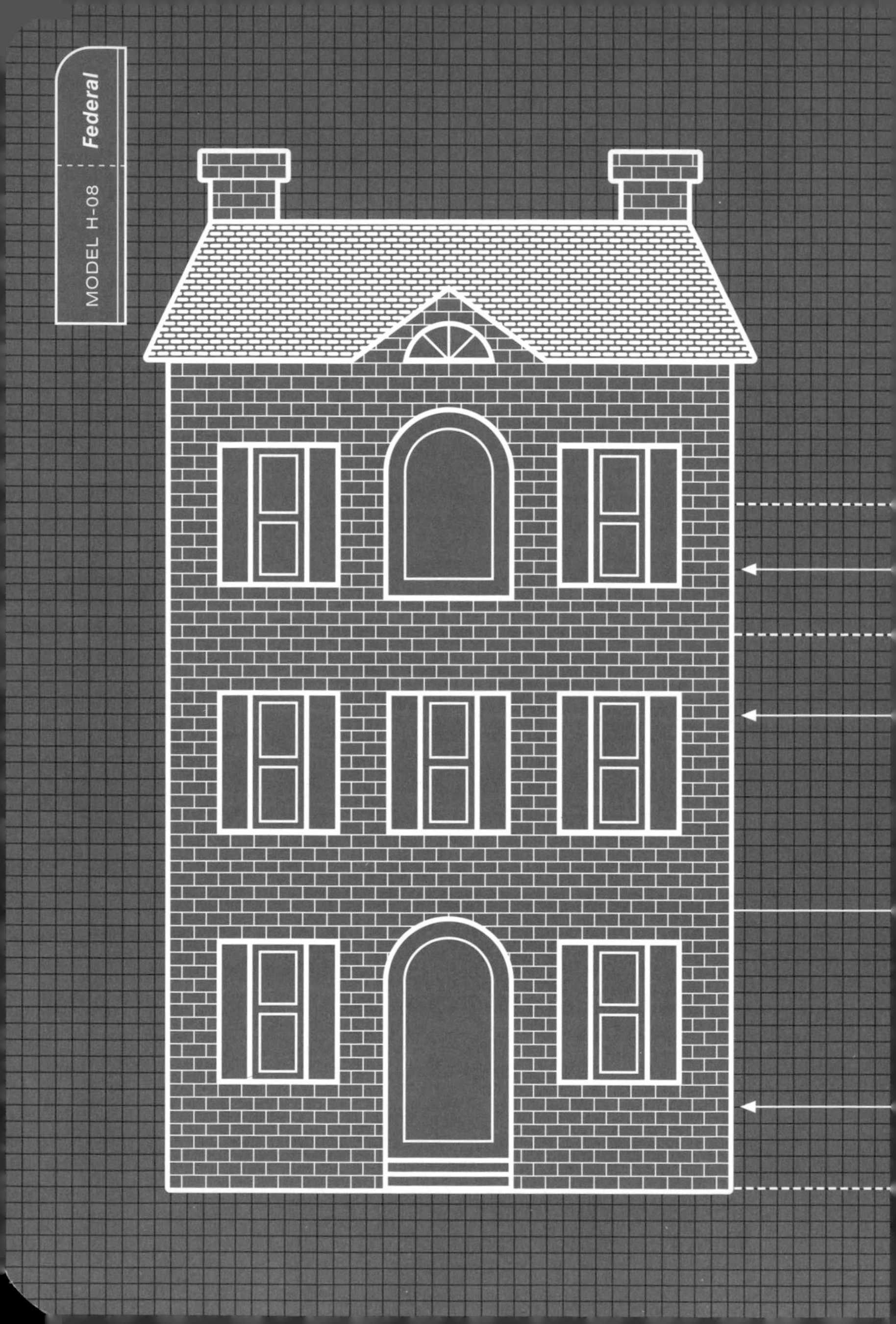
Federal
MODEL H-08

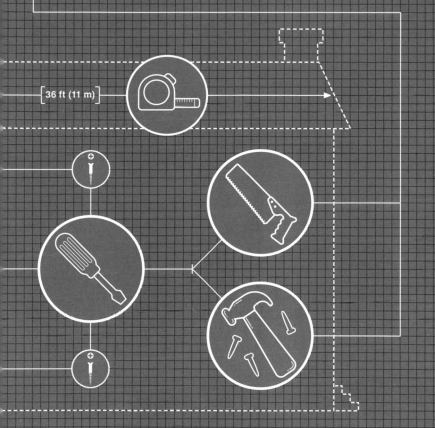

[Chapter 8]

Upgrades

[36 ft (11 m)]

Remodeling Benefits

Soon after home occupants are fully installed, they begin making a list of ideas for Home 2.0:

- Remodel the kitchen
- Remodel one or more bathrooms
- Remodel an extra room

They are upgrading their home. There are many excellent reasons for home upgrades, including commitment to remaining in the home, increased livability, and increased value.

Commitment to Remaining in the Home

Once home occupants make the commitment to purchase a house, the work begins. Moving in. Selecting furniture and appliances. Decorating. Maintaining and repairing. Making a house into a comfortable home. Installed occupants make financial, physical, and emotional investments in a specific residence and are rewarded with a better life. As the needs, desires, and abilities of occupants change, the home must respond or be replaced. Because replacing the home requires an extensive installation process, many homeowners decide to upgrade rather than move. The money saved by not moving may fund needed upgrades. In addition, home-owners can use the current home as equity for a remodeling loan.

Increased Livability

Homes serve the convenience of installed occupants. An unsuitable home may require replacement to be functional for all occupants, but most homes require upgrades only to make them more livable. For example, a home without sufficient storage for all occupants is easier to upgrade than to replace. It typically is easier to add a bathroom to an otherwise suitable home than to replace the home and relocate occupants. If occupants decide, however, that their current home just doesn't work for them anymore, or if there is a need to relocate, the family unit will engage in the search for a new home and a search for a buyer for the old home. This time, the family unit can use all the knowledge they have acquired through home ownership to find a more suitable dwelling to inhabit.

Increased Value

Homes are an excellent investment in most marketplaces, multiplying an initial outlay by returns difficult to match with other ventures. Increasing the expenditure for upgrades increases the total return. In addition, the occupants receive nonmonetary returns in increased livability. The caveat is making sure that the investment in upgrades offers a sufficient future financial return. Fortunately, well-planned upgrades in kitchens, bathrooms, and other primary rooms usually offer good returns on the investment, especially if homeowners keep costs reasonable by performing the upgrades themselves, or helping with the upgrades.

EXPERT TIP: Home equity *(difference between current value and mortgage balance) can be used as security for a second mortgage, often called a* remodeling loan*. The application process is similar to conventional financing (see page 63).*

Remodeling Basics

Remodeling is the alteration or revision of an existing residence. An addition appends an existing structure. Most home upgrades are remodels that involve changing what already is in place. Because of this, remodels typically are less expensive than additions.

⚠️ *CAUTION: Remodeling projects can be extensive. Instructions for remodeling in this chapter serve as guidelines only. See page 214 for additional resources.*

Planning

The key to all remodeling upgrades is planning. Poorly planned remodels cost more, take more time, and have less functionality than well-planned projects. The first step in planning an upgrade is defining what needs to be accomplished:

- What will the remodeled room do for installed occupants?
- What primary and secondary services will the remodeled room provide?
- Is the main function of the remodeled room to increase capacity, functionality, or aesthetics?
- What are the room's secondary and tertiary functions?
- What financial and time constraints limit the remodeling project?
- By how much will the remodeling project increase the home's economic value?
- What features do installed occupants (1) need and (2) want in the remodeled room(s)?

Once the goals and functions have been established for an upgraded room, planning begins. The purpose of a plan is to document the state, design, and requirements of the room for remodeling. Drawings are made of the existing room's state, overlaid with the proposed changes. Then requirements are listed, such as which components require removal or replacement and which are new components required by the design.

⚠ **EXPERT TIP:** *In most locations, remodeling projects require approval by a local authority before work can begin. Homeowners should contact the local building department to determine remodeling requirements, including plans and permits. Building codes are established for the safety and health of current and future occupants.*

Hiring

Once the homeowner understands the remodeling process for identified projects, the next question is "Who will perform the required labor?" Many homeowners hire remodeling contractors with specific experience with the planned project: kitchens, bathrooms, or other rooms. In addition, homeowners frequently hire architects to draft the remodeling plans that will guide the contractor or other laborer through the project.

Questions that homeowners should answer before hiring a contractor or architect include:

■ How extensive is the remodeling project; is it a facelift or a major overhaul of the room(s)?
■ How extensive do the remodeling plans need to be, and who can best produce these plans?

⚠ **EXPERT TIP:** *Home remodeling software programs are available that can make producing and printing plans relatively easy. Consumer versions* *of these programs are priced under $100 and are available at larger home centers and computer stores.*

■ Do occupants have the skills, time, and energy to learn how to perform and complete the remodeling project?
■ Does the homeowner have sufficient capital to hire contractors, or will the homeowner hire and supervise experienced craftspeople or occupant labor?

⚠ **CAUTION:** *Make sure that all agreements with contractors are in writing and signed by all parties. Contractors will develop a bid that includes the remodeling job description and costs, but any changes made require a separate change order and price.*

■ Can experienced friends or relatives be utilized in the remodeling project?
■ How motivated are the homeowner(s) and occupants to undertake the remodeling project without assistance?

💡 **EXPERT TIP:** *In many states, contractors are required to be licensed and bonded before performing any remodeling projects worth more than $500. In addition, licensed contractors must include their state license number on literature and contracts. Consumers may contact the state licensing board to determine status and whether complaints have been file on licensed contractors.*

Using Occupant Labor

For many remodeling projects, occupants can perform most if not all required tasks. If occupants lack experience, they can take classes or read books on the topic, whether it involves electrical systems, plumbing, flooring, and so forth. Alternatively, occupants can perform some of the tasks that require fewer skills, such as removing existing fixtures and painting. Professionals are then hired for skilled services, especially those that must meet local code requirements and pass an inspection before approval.

Many occupants find that performing various maintenance and repair projects (Chapters 4 through 6) offers sufficient training to attempt at least a portion of remodeling projects. In addition, larger remodeling components, such as uninstalling and reinstalling cabinets, can be learned from sales staff when buying ready-made cabinetry at home centers.

Remodeling a Kitchen

The most popular home upgrade is kitchen remodeling. Simple remodeling includes refinishing cabinets and replacing plumbing fixtures and appliances. More compete remodeling includes replacing flooring, plumbing, electrical and lighting systems, and cabinets and counters. The kitchen remodeling process begins with planning.

Planning

The planning of a kitchen remodel begins with documenting the room's state (what it looks like now). Then the new design is made and the change requirements are identified. To plan a kitchen remodel:

[1] Measure and record all room dimensions in pencil on grid paper or with a software program, including walls and windows, and the location of cabinets, plumbing fixtures, and electrical fixtures and appliances. Include all dimensions and add clarifying notations.

[2] Make a photocopy of (or save the file of) the current kitchen plan and note it as the current plan.

[3] Change the original plan to include fixtures and features proposed for the remodeled kitchen. Include notes on new flooring, cabinets, plumbing, electrical systems, and other components, identifying any required movement of plumbing or electrical components.

⚠ **EXPERT TIP:** *Local building codes will dictate the dimensions and placement of standard kitchen cabinetry. Standard cabinets are 18-, 36-, 48-, and 60-in (45.7-, 91.4-, 121.9-, and 152.4-cm) wide, with other widths available. Standard base cabinets are 36 in (91.4 cm) high and 25 in (63.5 cm) deep. Standard wall cabinets are 15 in (38.1 cm) deep and mounted 18 in (45.7 cm) above base cabinets. Custom cabinets may be of any width, depth, and height within building code limits.*

[4] Make a list of all required materials and components, called the *materials list*, for the kitchen remodeling project.

[5] Take the materials list to a builder's supplier, home center, remodeling store, or construction materials retailer for a bid on the costs of all components.

⚠ **EXPERT TIP:** *Contractors and architects typically perform the planning and bidding process for customers.*

Flooring

Installing new flooring materials is covered in Chapter 7 with brief instructions for installing hard tile and vinyl-composition tile, the two most popular materials for kitchen floors.

For remodeling projects, the existing flooring in many cases must be removed. Perimeter-fastened flooring is removed by first removing molding that covers the staples at the edge of the flooring, and then removing the staples. Some flooring uses adhesive to attach to the subfloor, requiring a heat gun and a large putty knife for removal. Alternatively, thin panels of backing or liquid floor leveling products can be installed over the existing flooring to provide a smooth surface for the new flooring.

⚠ **EXPERT TIP:** *Homeowners who are removing flooring don't have to be as careful as installers. Use a utility knife or a hammer and chisel as needed to break up and remove existing flooring. Be careful not to damage the sub-floor. For difficult floors, flooring removal tools can be rented at rental centers and some flooring shops.*

Plumbing

Simple kitchen remodeling projects may include replacement of primary plumbing fixtures, such as sinks and faucets, without moving their location. If plumbing fixtures are moved, water pipes and drains within the wall or floor may need to be moved as well, a more difficult task.

Typical water supply pipes are $3/4$-in (1.9-cm) diameter for both cold and hot water lines that run horizontally, with $1/2$-in (1.3-cm) pipe running vertically from supply lines to the fixtures. Kitchen sinks often have $1/4$-in (0.6 cm) lines from the wall to the faucet.

⚠ **EXPERT TIP:** *In some areas, manifold plumbing is used in newer homes with a manifold (one inlet with several outlets) just inside the home and separate $1/4$-in (0.6-cm) tubes running from it to each of the individual fixtures within the home. One advantage (besides cost savings) is offering a single location where any one or all water supply lines can be turned off in an emergency.*

PLANNING KITCHEN 2.0

1. Decide location of new plumbing fixtures.
2. Determine proper electrical voltage.
3. Utilize vertical space.

REMODELING A KITCHEN: Remodeling a kitchen is one of the most

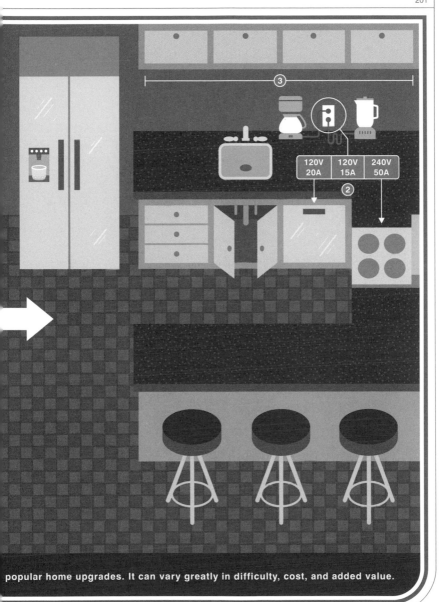

120V
20A

120V
15A

240V
50A

popular home upgrades. It can vary greatly in difficulty, cost, and added value.

Using the remodeling materials list, the homeowner or contractor can purchase each plumbing component for the job. Most large home centers offer workshops and classes on basic plumbing skills, including how to select and install pipe and fixtures. Also, most plumbing fixtures include basic installation instructions.

Electrical and Lighting

Replacing electrical fixtures is easy following instructions furnished with the fixtures. Rewiring a room, however, is more difficult and requires a licensed electrician or an experienced homeowner.

Dishwashers require 120 v and 20 amp service on a dedicated circuit. Electric ranges typically use 120 v service for lights and controls and 240 v service for the heating elements; amperage should be 50. All other kitchen circuits are 120 v and 15 amp (lighting) or 20 amp (appliance) service. Garbage disposers are powered through an electrical outlet under the sink, typically 20 amp. Once they have developed home maintenance experience, most installed occupants feel comfortable installing replacement built-in appliances following instructions included with the unit.

Cabinets and Counters

Kitchen cabinets can be replaced or refinished in place, removing doors and stripping or painting all surfaces without removing them from the walls. Countertops are attached from the underside to the cabinet frame and can be unscrewed. New laminate tops can be purchased and installed on existing cabinet frames for a new look to the kitchen. Alternatively, the top can be replaced with a sub-top of plywood, and ceramic tile can be installed, similar to hard tile installation on a subfloor (see page 188).

To install kitchen cabinets:

[**1**] Remove all old cabinetry and plumbing. If new flooring is to be installed, do so now.

[**2**] Measure and mark a point on the walls 34^1/$_2$ in (87.6 cm) above the floor. Use a line level and chalk line to mark a horizontal line at this point, the top of base cabinets.

[**3**] Measure and mark a point 49^1/$_2$ in (125.7 cm) above the chalk line (89 in or 213.3 cm above the floor). Use a line level and chalk line to mark a horizontal line at this point, the top of wall cabinets.

[**4**] Use a stud finder and pencil to mark the location of all wall studs, placing the mark above the 34^1/$_2$-in (87.6-cm) base cabinet line.

[**5**] Starting with a corner cabinet, use a level to position the first cabinet, then use a screw gun and screws to loosely fasten the cabinet back to wall studs.

[**6**] Continue installing cabinets to the wall, working around the room.

[**7**] Once all wall cabinets are in place, use shims to level the front of each cabinet, and then fasten them more securely to the wall and to adjacent cabinets.

[**8**] Install the wall cabinets following the same instructions.

⚠ *EXPERT TIP: For some remodeling jobs, it may be easier to install wall cabinets before installing base cabinets.*

To install base cabinet counter tops:

[**1**] Measure the base cabinet top.

[**2**] If installing a prefabricated top, cut the top to fit the base with a 1-in (2.5-cm) overhang at all edges. If installing a ceramic tile countertop, cut the sub-top to the base cabinet measurements with a $1/2$-in (1.3-cm) overhang.

[**3**] Carefully place and position the prefabricated countertop on the counter, and fasten the cabinet to the top from underneath using screws through the cabinet corner blocks. Apply adhesive to ceramic tiles and install tile and grout.

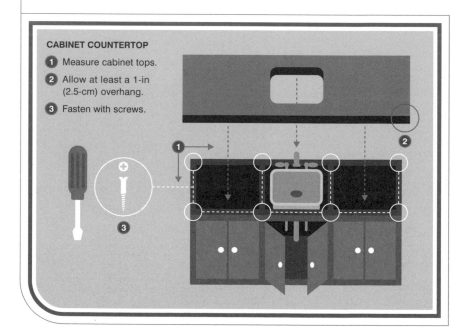

CABINET COUNTERTOP
1. Measure cabinet tops.
2. Allow at least a 1-in (2.5-cm) overhang.
3. Fasten with screws.

Remodeling a Bathroom

Bathroom remodels are similar to kitchen remodels, except for fixtures. Bathroom remodels may require the replacement or installation of a new bathtub, shower, or other bathing device. Bathroom remodeling jobs typically require more plumbing and less electrical work than kitchen remodels.

Planning

The planning of a bathroom remodel begins with a drawing of the room, followed by a drawing of proposed changes. To plan a bathroom remodel:

[**1**] Measure and record all room dimensions in pencil on grid paper or with a software program, including walls, windows, as well as the location of cabinets, plumbing fixtures, and electrical fixtures and appliances. Include all dimensions and add clarifying notations.

[**2**] Make a photocopy of (or save the file of) the current kitchen plan and note it as the original plan.

[**3**] Change the original plan to include fixtures and features proposed for the remodeled bathroom. Include notes on new flooring, cabinets, plumbing, electrical, and other components, identifying any required movement of plumbing or electrical components.

EXPERT TIP: Local building codes will dictate the dimensions and placement of standard bathroom fixtures. Standard bathtubs are 32 in (81.3 cm) wide by 60 in (152.4 cm) long. The space required for standard toilets is an area 30 in (76.2 cm) wide and 50 in (127 cm) deep, though the fixture is smaller. Standard shower stalls are 36 in (91.4 cm) square; small stalls are

32 in (81.3 cm) square. Custom fixtures may be of any width, depth, and height within building code limits.

[4] Make a list of all required materials and components, called the *materials list*, for the bathroom remodeling project.

[5] Take the materials list to a builder's supplier, home center, remodeling store, or other construction materials retailer for a bid on the costs of all components.

Flooring

Bathroom flooring must stand up to more moisture than other rooms, so selection and installation are critical. Most bathrooms do not use hardwood or carpet flooring for this reason. Instead, most installations are of hard tile or VCT (see pages 185–189).

⚠️ *EXPERT TIP: Bathroom subflooring may be damaged by excess moisture and require repair or replacement during a thorough remodeling job. Carefully inspect the condition of subflooring at the edges of the bathtub, shower, and toilet. If unresolved, bathroom moisture problems can cause problems in rooms below or next to the bathroom.*

Cabinets and Counters

Bathroom cabinets can be replaced following installation instructions for kitchen cabinets (see pages 203–204 for step-by-step instructions). Alternatively, they can be refinished in place, removing doors and stripping or painting all surfaces without removing them from the walls. Countertops are attached to the cabinet frame from the underside. Laminate tops can be installed on new or existing cabinet frames. Ceramic tops can be installed on bathroom cabinets similar to hard tile installation on a subfloor (see page 185).

Because bathrooms typically are smaller than kitchens, the size, location, and clearance of cabinets is more critical. Careful planning and installation are essential. Local building codes dictate clearances to allow safe access to all primary fixtures, including tubs and toilets. Information on code requirements is available at local building departments and from some home centers.

Plumbing

The easiest bathroom remodels are those that do not require replacement or moving of primary plumbing fixtures, such as tubs, showers, toilets, and lavatories. Replacing fixtures is easier than moving plumbing. If plumbing fixtures are moved, they require that water pipes and drains within the wall or floor are moved as well. For these tasks, most homeowners call a professional plumber.

As with other rooms with water service, water supply pipes in bathrooms are $3/4$-in (1.9 cm) diameter for both cold and hot water lines that run horizontally, with $1/2$-in (1.3 cm) pipe running vertically from supply lines to the fixtures. Bathroom toilets and lavatories have $1/4$-in (0.6-cm) lines from the wall to the fixture.

Refer to the bathroom remodeling materials list when shopping for components.

Electrical and Lighting

Because bathrooms use water, a superior conductor of electricity, planning for safe bathroom electrical and lighting systems is crucial. Especially important is the installation of grounding systems that offer electricity a route to ground instead of occupants.

Replacing electrical fixtures is easy following instructions furnished with the fixtures. Rewiring a room, however, is more difficult and requires a licensed electrician or an experienced homeowner. Most bathroom circuits are 120 v with 15 amp (lighting) or 20 amp (appliance) service.

Remodeling an Extra Room

Upgrading a home to version 2.0 (or at least 1.1) may require remodeling a living room, dining room, family room, or bedroom for new use. Because these rooms don't include major appliances or plumbing, they are easier to modify. In most cases, remodeling simply means removing all current components, decorating as desired, and installing new components. The components are portable and can be installed in any selected room of the appropriate size and location. Rooms can be remodeled to serve as:

- Home office
- Media room
- Entertainment center
- Music room
- Nursery
- Apartment for elders
- Game room
- Party room
- Storage room
- Craft room
- Home gym
- Spiritual room
- Teen apartment
- Two or more of the above functions

The process for remodeling an existing room for new functions is similar to that for remodeling kitchens and bathrooms: plan, uninstall, decorate, and install. Even garages can be converted into extra rooms following these guidelines.

Planning

Developing plans for a room that is changing functions is relatively easy. The primary task is determining if the new purpose can be served by the size and location of the room. A dining room may be the appropriate size for a home office, but may not be in the best location due to proximity to active living areas.

⚠ *CAUTION: Locating a home office near a kitchen may be hazardous to the dietary health of home workers. If possible, locate work areas far away from eating areas.*

In addition, the room to be remodeled must have the services required by the new purpose. For example, a media room needs cable television or satellite service as well as sufficient electrical service. A teen apartment requires access to a nearby bathroom, preferably one that is dedicated.

Uninstalling

To modify a room's function, some or all of the portable components within the room must be moved to another location within the home or otherwise disposed of. A spare bedroom that is being remodeled into a spiritual room, for example, will require that the bed and other furnishings be moved, stored, sold, or donated.

INTERIOR DESIGN TIPS

1. Determine space required.
2. Decide which services are needed.
3. Uninstall obsolete furniture.
4. Decorate room to taste.
5. Install new furniture and/or equipment.

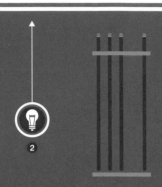

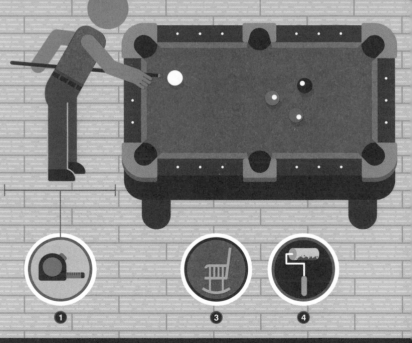

REMODELING AN EXTRA ROOM: The remodeling process can be

093005

GAME OVER

broken down into four steps: planning, uninstalling, decorating, and installing.

Decorating

To fully serve the room's new function it should be decorated (see Chapter 7). The process includes painting, installing wall covering, and installing or upgrading flooring. Once components from the room's previous function have been uninstalled, it will be easier to visualize and redecorate the bare room. The new function(s) may dictate the selection of colors and styles. Allow the new room's primary user to assist in selecting and decorating the room.

Installing

Finally, components for the new function are installed in the room. Electrical receptacles and switches should be added or moved prior to decorating. As needed, additional service such as computer network or television cabling must be installed in the same manner as electrical wiring and receptacles. New components include furniture, fixtures, portable lighting, and supplies.

⚠ *EXPERT TIP: Anticipate what future uses the room may serve, and consider incorporating some of the components as the new room is installed.*

Once the room is planned, decorated, and installed, occupants may utilize the functional space for the designed activities. Planning for Home 2.1 may begin soon thereafter.

[Appendix]

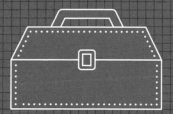

Technical Support

The following resources offer valuable information and/or services to homeowners:

 Fix-It Club® www.fixitclub.com

Online illustrated instructions for fixing more than 125 household components, including structural, electrical, plumbing, heating, cooling, and security systems; written by Dan and Judy Ramsey.

American Homeowner
Resource Center
www.ahrc.com
(949) 366-2125
Online resource for members of home-owner associations to help preserve, strengthen, and enrich the American home.

Bob Vila
www.bobvila.com
Online resource for home decorating and construction from Bob Vila of *Home Again* television show.

Danny Lipford
www.dannylipford.com
Includes how-to articles and resources for homeowners on home improvement, maintenance, and repair by the host of *Today*'s homeowner program.

DoItYourself.com
www.doityourself.com
Provides instructions for do-it-your-selfers on a variety of home projects.

Homeownernet.com
www.homeownernet.com
Offers information and tips on home maintenance and remodeling.

Hometime
www.hometime.com
Online resource for home improvement, remodeling, and repair information from Dean Johnson of *Hometime* television show.

The Money Pit
www.moneypit.com
Home improvement radio show featuring Tom Kraeutler and Leslie Segrete

Glossary of Terms

■ **Amortization:** The building of equity and reduction of debt through regular monthly payments of principal and interest.

■ **Bearing wall:** A wall that supports any vertical load in addition to its own weight.

■ **Building code:** The collection of legal requirements for the construction of buildings.

■ **Circuit:** The path of electric current as it travels from the source to the appliance or fixture and back to the source.

■ **Circuit breaker:** A safety device used to interrupt the flow of power when the electricity exceeds a predetermined amount. Unlike a fuse, a circuit breaker can be reset.

■ **CPVC (chlorinated polyvinyl chloride):** The rigid white or pastel-colored plastic pipe used for water supply lines.

■ **Current:** The movement or flow of electrons, which provides electric power. The rate of electron flow is measured in amperes (amps).

■ **Drywall:** Panels consisting of a layer of gypsum plaster covered on both sides with paper, used for finishing interior walls and ceilings. Also called *wallboard*, *gypsum wallboard*, and *Sheetrock*, a trade name.

■ **DWV (drain-waste-vent):** An acronym referring to all or part of the plumbing system that carries waste water from fixtures to the sewer and gases to the roof.

■ **Fixture:** In plumbing, any device that is permanently attached to the water system of a house. In electrical work, any lighting device attached to the surface, recessed into, or hanging from the ceiling or walls.

■ **Foundation:** The supporting portion of a structure below the first-floor construction or below grade.

■ **Fuse:** A safety device for electrical circuits; interrupts the flow of current when it exceeds predetermined limits for a specific time period.

■ **Ground:** Connected to the earth or something serving as the earth, such as a cold-water pipe. The ground wire in an electrical circuit is usually bare or has green insulation.

■ **Hot wire:** In an electrical circuit, any wire that carries current from the power source to an electrical device. The hot wire is usually identified with black, blue, or red insulation, but it can be any color but white or green.

■ **Junction box:** A metal or plastic container for electrical connections. Sometimes called a *box*.

■ **Lath:** A building material of metal, gypsum, wood, or other material; used as a base for plaster or stucco.

■ **Loan-to-value (LTV) ratio:** The relationship between the amount of a mortgage loan and the value of the property.

■ **Mortgage:** An agreement between a lender and a buyer using real property as security for the loan.

■ **Neutral wire:** In a circuit, any wire that is kept at zero voltage. The neutral wire completes the circuit from source to fixture or appliance to ground. The covering of neutral wires is always white.

■ **Nominal size:** The size designation of a piece of lumber before it is planed or surfaced. If the actual size of a piece of surfaced lumber is $1\frac{1}{2}$ by $3\frac{1}{2}$ in, it is referred to by its nominal size: 2 by 4.

■ **Nonbearing wall:** A wall supporting no load other than its own weight.

■ **Penny:** As applied to nails, originally indicated the price per hundred. The term now serves as a measure of nail length and is abbreviated by the letter *d*.

■ **Pitch:** The incline of a roof.

■ **PITI:** An acronym for principal, interest, taxes, and insurance.

■ **Principal and interest:** The monthly cost of a mortgage; principal is the amount borrowed (the difference between the cost of the home and the down payment) while interest is the charge made by the lender for lending the money.

■ **PVC (polyvinyl chloride):** A rigid, white, plastic pipe used in plumbing for supply and DWV systems.

■ **Receptacle:** In a wall, ceiling, or floor, an electric device into which the plugs on appliance and extension cords are placed to connect them to electric power. Also called an *outlet*.

■ **Riser:** Each of the vertical boards between the treads of a stairway.

■ **Service panel:** The box or panel where the electricity is distributed to the house circuits. It contains the circuit breakers or fuses and, usually, the main disconnect switch.

■ **Sheathing:** Sheet material or boards fastened to the rafters or exterior stud walls, to which the roofing or siding is applied.

■ **Shutoff valve:** In plumbing, a fitting to shut off the water supply to a single fixture or branch of pipe.

■ **Stud:** One of a series of wood or metal vertical framing members that are the main units of walls and partitions.

■ **Subfloor:** Plywood or oriented strand board (OSB) attached to the joists. The finish floor is laid over the subfloor.

■ **Switch:** In electrical systems, a device for turning the flow of electricity on and off in a circuit or diverting the current from one circuit to another.

■ **Tread:** In a stairway, the horizontal surface on which a person steps.

■ **Vapor barrier:** Any material used to prevent the penetration of water vapor into walls or other enclosed parts of a building. Polyethylene sheets, aluminum foil, and building paper are the materials used most often.

■ **Wall plate:** A decorative covering for a switch, receptacle, or other device.

Index

A

A-Frame style, 33
accessibility, 38–39
adaptive reuse, 37
apartments, 30, 43, 46–47
appliances, fixing, 151–52
attic water stains, 126–27

B

ball faucets, repairing, 154–55
basement leaks, 161
bathroom remodeling, 205–208
Beaux-Arts style, 32

C

cabinets and counters
    bathrooms, 206–207
    kitchen, 202–204
Cape Cod style, 31
carpets
    installing, 182–83, 186
    maintaining, 94–95
cartridge faucets, repairing, 154–55
ceilings, 73
chimney cleaning, 114–15
circuit breakers, 103–104
cleaning
    chimneys, 114–15
    ductwork, 111–12
    garage floors, 143–44
    gutters, 127
    heating and cooling filters, 112–13
    humidifiers and dehumidifiers, 116
    radiators, 117
    siding, 128–30

structural maintenance, 93–94
closing on a home, 60–62
Colonial Revival style, 32
component moving services, 67
compression faucets, repairing, 155
concrete, patching, 144
condominium apartments, 30, 43, 46–47
contractors, 189
cooling. See heating and cooling emergencies; heating and cooling maintenance; heating and cooling system
cooperative apartments, 30, 43, 46–47
cords, electrical, 101, 103
counters. See cabinets and counters
Craftsman style, 33, 34
cultural upgrades, 39

D

decks, 134–38
    diagram, 136–37
    pressure washing, 134–35
    recoating, 135, 138
decorating, 170, 212
dehumidifiers, cleaning, 116
design philosophy, 27
dimensions, home, 26–27
distressed homes, 53
Dome style, 33
doors and windows
    door locks, 95–96
    garages, 145
    interior painting, 176
    outdoor storage structures, 142–43
    overview, 73
    recaulking, 133
    weather stripping, 132

window seals, 133–34

drains
clogged bathroom, 157, 158–59
clogged kitchen, 156–58
slow, 105–106
drives, 139–40
ductwork cleaning, 111–12

E
Earth style, 31
electrical power, restoring, 152–54
electrical system, 74–78
bathroom, 207–208
diagram, 76–77
emergencies, 151–54
kitchen, 202
maintenance, 100–105
maintenance materials, 85
overview, 18
emergency drills, 120–21
emergency repairs, 148–67
avoiding emergencies, 148
electrical emergencies, 151–54
heating and cooling emergencies, 164–67
plumbing emergencies, 154–63
structural emergencies, 148–51
environmentally friendly design, 36
exterior maintenance. See maintenance, exterior
exterior painting, 131–32

F
fasteners and tools, 86–88
faucets, repairing, 154–55
Federal style, 31
feng shui, 39
filters, heating and cooling, 112–13
financing, 63–64
fire extinguishers, 118–19
fixtures, checking for leaks, 106–107

floor cleaning, garage, 143–44
floor plans, 38
flooring
bathroom, 206
carpeting, 182–83, 186
hard tile, 185, 187, 188
hardwood flooring, 183–84, 187
kitchen, 198–99
overview, 71
vinyl-composition tile, 188–89
Folk Victorian style, 32
foundations, 70
Foursquare style, 32, 35
French style, 33
FSBOs (for sale by owner), 60
fuel leaks, 164
functional spaces, 25
fuses, 103–104

G
garages, 143–45
general contractors, 180
Georgian Colonial style, 31, 34
glossary of terms, 215–17
Greek Revival style, 31, 35
ground-fault circuit-interrupters (GFCIs),
104–105
gutter cleaning, 127

H
hard tile installation, 185, 187, 188
hardware stores, 88–89
hardwood flooring, installing, 183–84, 187
health-conscious designs, 37
heating and cooling emergencies, 164–67
heating and cooling maintenance, 110–18
bleeding air from hot water heating
systems, 118
checking fans, belts, and motors, 113

cleaning chimneys, 114–15
cleaning ductwork, 111–12
cleaning humidifiers and dehumidifiers, 116
cleaning or replacing filters, 112–13
cleaning radiators, 117
inspecting systems, 110–11
heating and cooling system
    diagram, 81
    maintenance materials, 86
    no cooling, 165–67
    no heating, 164–65
    overview, 20–21, 80–82
help, professional, 189
hinges, maintaining, 142–43
history of homes, 24
home condition, 52–57
    distressed homes, 53
    inspection checklist, 54–57
    new homes, 52, 53
    pre-owned homes, 52, 53
home design trends, 36–39
home styles, 31–36
humidifier cleaning, 116

I

inspection checklist, 54–57
interior maintenance. *See* maintenance, interior
interior painting. *See* painting, interior
investment opportunities, 28

K

kitchen remodeling, 197–204
    cabinets and counters, 202–204
    diagrams, 200–201
    electrical and lighting, 202
    flooring, 198–99
    planning, 197–98
    plumbing, 199, 202

L

leaks
    basement, 161
    checking pipes and fixtures for, 106–107
    faucet, 154–55
    fuel, 164
    water heater, 163
life span of homes, 21
location, choosing, 50–51
locks, door, 95–96
Log style, 31

M

maintenance
    benefits of, 83–84
    materials for, 84–86
maintenance, exterior, 124–45
    decks, 134–38
    doors and windows, 132–34
    garages, 143–45
    outdoor storage structures, 142–43
    patios, walks, and drives, 139–40
    roofing, 125–27
    siding, 128–30
    tree maintenance, 141
    yard maintenance, 140–41
maintenance, interior, 92–121
    electrical maintenance, 100–105
    heating and cooling maintenance, 110–18
    plumbing maintenance, 105–109
    safety maintenance, 118–21
    structural maintenance, 93–100
Mission style, 32, 34
moving in, 64–67

N

Neoeclectic style, 33
new homes, 52, 53

O

off-site construction, 36–37
outdoor living, 39
outdoor storage structures, 142–43
ownership
    advantages of, 28
    disadvantages of, 29
    options, 29–30

P

painting, exterior, 131–32
painting, interior, 170–78
    cleaning up, 177–78
    overview, 96–99
    paint types, 172–73
    painting tools, 174–75
    preparing surfaces, 170–72
    process, 176–77
patching
    concrete, 144
    patios, walks, and drives, 140
patios, walks, and drives, 139–40
paying for a home, 62–64
pipes
    broken, 160–61
    checking for leaks, 106–107
planned-unit developments, 30, 43, 45
plumbing
    bathroom remodeling, 207
    diagram, 79
    kitchen remodeling, 199, 202
    maintenance, 105–109
    maintenance materials, 85–86
    overview, 19, 78–80
plumbing emergencies, 154–63
    broken pipes, 160–61
    clogged bathroom drain, 157, 158–59
    clogged kitchen drain, 156–58
    clogged toilet, 159–60

    leaky basement, 161
    leaky faucet, 154–55
    leaky water heater, 163
    no hot water, 162–63
Prairie style, 33
pre-owned homes, 52, 53
pressure washing
    decks, 134–35
    patios, walks, and drives, 139
professional help, 189
Pueblo Revival style, 33

R

radiator cleaning, 117
Ranch style, 33, 35
real estate agents, 58–59
recaulking doors and windows, 133
receptacles, electrical, 100–101, 102
remodeling
    bathrooms, 205–8
    benefits of, 192–93
    extra rooms, 208–12
    hiring, 195–96
    planning, 194–95
    using occupant labor, 196–97
    See also kitchen remodeling
residence types, 43–48
resources and technical support, 214
reverse-compression faucets, repairing, 155
roofing
    maintaining, 125–27
    overview, 73–74
    repairing, 150–51

S

safety maintenance, 118–21
security, 83
self moves, 65–66
Shingle style, 32

shopping
  in hardware stores, 88–89
  for a home, 58–62
siding
  cleaning, 128–30
  damaged, 148–49
  inspecting for pests and damage, 130
  outdoor storage structures, 142
  painting, 131–32
  recaulking, 133
single-family residences, 29, 43, 44
smoke detector testing, 120
Southern Colonial style, 31, 34
Split-Entry style, 33, 35
stairs, 71
storage, 39
storage structures, outdoor, 142–43
structural components, 15–17
structural emergencies, 148–51
structural maintenance, 93–100
  cleaning, 93–94
  filling surface holes, 99–100
  maintaining carpets, 94–95
  maintaining door locks, 95–96
  materials, 84
  painting interior, 96–99
surface holes, filling, 99–100
survival pantry replenishment, 121
switches, electrical, 100–101, 102

T

tax advantages, 28
technical support, 214
toilets, clogged, 159–60
tools and fasteners, 86–88
tree maintenance, 141
Tudor style, 32, 35

U

usage, determining, 48–50

V

vastu shastra, 39
Victorian Gothic style, 32, 34
Victorian Queen Anne style, 32
vinyl-composition tile installation, 188–89

W

walks, 139–40
wall coverings, 179–82
wallpaper, installing, 180–82
walls, 71–72
water heaters
  draining sludge from, 107–108
  leaky, 163
  testing relief valve, 108–109
weather resistance, 38
weather stripping, 132
window seals, 133–34
windows. *See* doors and windows
wood, rotten or eaten, 149–50

Y

yard maintenance, 140–41

OWNER'S CERTIFICATE

Congratulations! Now that you've studied all the instructions in this manual, you are fully prepared to maintain your home. With proper care and attention, your model will provide you with many years of livability. Enjoy!

Owner's name

_____

Model's location

_____

Model's style

_____

Model's date of acquisition

_____

Occupant installation date

_____

Notes

_____

_____

About the Authors:

DAN RAMSEY is a licensed building and home improvement contractor who has taught thousands of homeowners how to fix things through more than two dozen books and his **FIX-IT CLUB**® (www.FixItClub.com). Previously, he was a successful real estate agent. In addition, Dan has owned and maintained seven homes, including his latest at the gateway to the Redwoods in northern California. He currently is president of the National Association of Home & Workshop Writers (www.nahww.org). Dan lives and works with his wife and editor of 35 years, Judy. They have three children (Heather, Byron, and Brendon), three grandchildren, three pets, and three vehicles. Life is good!

About the Illustrators:

PAUL KEPPLE and **JUDE BUFFUM** are better known as the Philadelphia-based studio **HEADCASE DESIGN**. Their work has been featured in many design and illustration publications, such as *American Illustration, Communication Arts*, and *Print*. Paul worked at Running Press Book Publishers for several years before opening Headcase in 1998. Both graduated from the Tyler School of Art, where they now teach.